THE
ELEMENTS
OF
PERSUASION

Richard Maxwell and Robert Dickman

THE
ELEMENTS
OF
PERSUASION

Use Storytelling to Pitch Better, Sell Faster & Win More Business

Collins

An Imprint of HarperCollinsPublishers

HarperCollins books may be purchased for educational, business, or sales promotional use. For information, please write: Special Markets Department, HarperCollins Publishers, 10 East 53rd Street, New York, NY 10022.

FIRST EDITION

Designed by Kathryn Parise.

Library of Congress Cataloging-in-Publication Data

Dickman, Robert.
    The Elements of persuasion : use storytelling to pitch better, sell faster & win more business / Robert Dickman and Richard Maxwell. — 1st ed.
        p. cm.
    Includes index.
    ISBN: 978-0-06-117903-7
    1. Selling. 2. Persuasion (Psychology) 3. Success in business—Psychological aspects. 4. Business communication. 5. Storytelling. I. Maxwell, Richard. II. Title

    HF5438.25.D536 2007
    658.85—dc22

2007014567

07 08 09 10 11   ID/RRD   10 9 8 7 6 5 4 3 2 1

Dedicated to Oscar Ichazo

ACKNOWLEDGMENTS

When you are working with the five elements, it is amazing how often the number five turns up. There are five people without whose help and understanding this book would have been impossible. Our agent, Sarah Dickman, who was the spark that got us started and has kept things simmering nicely ever since; our editor, Sarah Brown, who "got" the book and helped us get it right and whose warmth and understanding has been the heart and soul of the editing process; our copy editor, Jim Gullickson, who spent hours toiling over our sometimes overheated prose catching errors of grammar or fact that would have made us look like even bigger boneheads than we actually are; and our wives, Aimee Levine Dickman and Christine Maxwell, for, well, being our wives, reading all of our drafts, and in general putting up with us. And of course we need to thank the one guy without whom this couldn't have happened, our publisher at HarperCollins, Marion Maneker, for believing in the book, holding our feet to the fire, and coming up with some great ideas when the clock was ticking. Thank you all.

CONTENTS

CHAPTER ONE

So What's Your Story?

There are two things everyone in business does every day. We all sell something—our products, our services, our skills, our ideas, our vision of where our business is going—and we tell stories. We sell things because that is how we as a democratic, capitalist society organize our energy. We tell stories because, as cognitive psychology is continuing to discover, stories are how we as human beings organize our minds. If we want to sell something, we have to persuade someone else to buy it.

We didn't always put such a high premium on persuasion. There was a time when the biggest and toughest among us simply told the smaller and more delicate what to do and punched them in the nose if that were a problem. Everyone, with the possible exception of Mike Tyson, agrees our modern way is better. But it has required us to learn a whole new skill set.

Compared with our great-grandparents, even the least skilled among us are crackerjack salespeople. It comes from practice.

One hundred years ago we didn't get much. Most of us lived on more or less self-contained farms. Our business was agriculture, controlled by slow seasonal rhythms. We sold our harvest once or twice a year. We got the market price. We hitched up our buckboard and rode into town once or twice a month and shopped at the general store. What we got there was largely generic. We wanted biscuits, but the type of biscuit we got was the type the store sold. Limited shelf space and the difficulties of transportation made brand options rare. We might try a new product, if the store clerk took the time to tell us how it was improved and how many satisfied customers he had, or we might not. Then, having completed our relatively intense commercial experience—intense enough so that going to the store was considered not a chore but entertainment—we headed back to our farm and our normal daily routine, secure in the knowledge that for the next week or so we wouldn't have to either buy or sell anything.

This left us easy marks for anyone who really knew how to deliver a sales pitch. Which is one of the reasons traveling salesmen got the reputation they got—and why some of us still feel slightly embarrassed about "being in sales." When the telephone reached out to even the most distant farms we resented it and called the salesmen who used this new medium to catch us around the dinner table "phonies." The name stuck.

Admittedly things weren't so leisurely paced if you lived in the slums of New York, and if you are reading this in Europe you will have to adjust the dates back one or two hundred years, but you get the idea. Buying and selling used to be an occasional thing.

Compare that with how many times you were involved in a sales pitch just on your way to work today. The newspaper ads your eyes skimmed past (but which had their subliminal effect), the radio spots that interrupted the news on your morning drive, the focus-group-tested sound bites the politicians used to push their parties' agendas (or, if your radio tastes are different, the product-placement mentions of burgers and beverages by your favorite rap artist), the billboards, the bumper stickers, the product logos on T-shirts. And they aren't just selling products. They are selling ideas, opinions, brand loyalties, political affiliations—you name it. Persuasion is very big business.

How big? In 1999, economist Deirdre McCloskey, writing in the *American Economic Review,* estimated that 28 percent of the GNP of the United States was involved in commercial persuasion. This includes law, public relations, the ministry, psychology, and marketing. That means last year almost $3.3 trillion was spent in the United States on commercial persuasion—selling.

Think about that—*$3.3 trillion.* That makes the "country of persuaders" the third-largest economy in the world.

To deal with all that persuasive pressure, to have even a

few meager dollars in our pockets at the end of the day, we have all had to develop tremendous sales resistance. To keep from being overwhelmed and paralyzed by all the demands that we do this or buy that, we have developed thick skins and the ability to ignore most of the chatter. For those of us whose business depends on being able to persuade others—which is all of us in business—the key to survival is being able to cut through all that clutter and make the sale.

The good news is that the secret of selling is what it has always been—a good story. It's that simple. Stories sell.

The even better news is that storytelling is innate in the human psyche. It is something we all know how to do.

In fact, it is so hardwired into us that it has its own place on our genome—a gene called *FOXP2*. Discovered in 2001 by Professor Anthony Monaco and his research team at Oxford University, *FOXP2* is now thought to be only the first of what scientists believe is a whole constellation of genes that make language and narrative possible. *FOXP2* specifically makes possible the subtle physical and neurological skills needed to speak words rapidly and precisely, and is probably linked to the use of complex syntax as well. From a cellular level on up, we are all born storytellers.

So if we all can tell stories, and stories are crucial to selling, why are some of us better at selling our products and ideas than others?

It's a lot like running. We all know how to do it, but only a few of us will ever break a four-minute mile. What separates the great runners from the also-rans is that great runners understand how to run *from the inside out*. They know how every stride, every muscle in that stride, fits together to achieve the goal. If we want to excel at persuasion, we need to understand story that same way.

The problem is that we are bombarded by so many stories every day—stories about what toothpaste is best, about terrorists lurking in the shadows, about new scientific discoveries and eternal spiritual truths—that it is hard to focus on story as story. To see a story for what it is rather than what it is about. We need to get stories to hold still long enough for us to get a good look at them. For that, we need a good definition.

The definition we will use throughout this book is a simple one:

A story is a fact, wrapped in an emotion that compels us to take an action that transforms our world.

In the early 1970s Jerome Bruner, one of the fathers of modern cognitive psychology, was closely observing very young children. He noticed, and soon proved, that even before children are able to talk they are organizing their world and communicating by simple stories.

First are what he called the stories of completion. The young child says (by means of gesture and facial expression), "All gone," when the bottle is empty. The child says, "Uh-oh," when she feels she has made a mistake and "Ohh!" when surprised or pleased.

These stories are short but complete. And they meet our definition. Take "All gone." The fact is that the bottle is empty. The baby wraps this fact in an emotion—either satisfaction or desire for more—and expresses that. Depending on which emotion is expressed, the parent is compelled to take an action—either to burp the baby and settle her down, or to get another bottle. Either way, the baby's world has been transformed for the better. Bruner went on to assert that infants develop meaning through narrative, and that the need to create stories precedes language. He even suggests that infants are motivated to learn to speak precisely because they already have stories inside themselves that they want to share with others.

In 1981 Bruner was involved in another study that extended these ideas. This one centered on a two-year-old girl known as "Emily." Emily's parents, university professors, noticed that when they put her to bed she spent time talking to herself before going to sleep. If you have kids you probably have noticed the same thing. Curious, Emily's parents put a microrecorder in her room and occasionally taped her monologues for the next eighteen months. The tapes (122 in total) were then given to a group of linguists and psychologists led by Harvard's Katherine Nelson, who discusses this research in her classic book *Narratives from the Crib*.

What Emily was doing in her room alone after her parents left wasn't pleasant babbling. She was mulling over the exciting events of her day, which was to be expected, but she was also projecting out, sometimes in great detail, what she would be doing tomorrow, who she would be doing it with, and how she might be feeling about it. In business terms, she was engaged in scenario planning, and she was doing it with an often wry sense of humor.

Bruner and the other researchers realized that Emily wasn't just using story to communicate with others. She was using it to shape and mold her own view of reality as well. Though Emily may have been more verbal than most, what she was doing is something we all did at her age as we drifted off to sleep—and what we all still do, though we might not be aware of it. She was weaving together the strands of her day into the fabric of her memory, and in doing that she was shaping the mental lens through which she would view each succeeding day. And she was doing it through the power of story.

So story is not simply the content of what we think, *it is also the how of how we think*. It is one of the key organizing principles of our mind.

There are three things that we should take away from Bruner's research for now.

1. Stories don't have to be long.
2. Stories don't have to be verbal.
3. The right story, at the right time, helps us shape and control our world.

The "George Bush at Ground Zero" story is a good example of all three points.

On September 14, 2001, President Bush visited the site of the 9/11 tragedy. He moved through the crowd of rescue workers who were still hoping to find the bodies of some of the nearly three thousand people who had died when the World Trade Center towers collapsed three days earlier. He climbed over the rubble, talking to workers, then he put an arm around the shoulders of a fireman who was wearing a white helmet, offering him a few words of hope. Someone handed the president a bullhorn. He stood up on a piece of the fallen tower and spoke briefly to the crowd. What he said was heartfelt but not often remembered. What is unforgettable is the image of the president standing in the rubble, his arm around a fireman, speaking to the crowd with calm, forceful resolve. That image, sometimes reduced to a single frame of video and put on the front page of a hundred newspapers, *is* the story.

It meets our definition. The fact is that the World Trade Center was destroyed by a terrorist attack, and this is conveyed clearly in every camera angle. By placing his arm around the fireman the president has wrapped that fact in a mix of simple but extremely powerful emotions—compassion, respect for the sacrifice of those who died going to the aid of others, clear resolve that this sacrifice would not be in vain. And in hindsight this image was the moment when the nation came out of its collective sense of shock and made up its mind to do something. When everything changed.

That is the power of the right story at the right time.

Now that we have a workable definition of what a story is, we can turn to this book's core questions: What makes a good story? What makes a story great? What gives a story staying power at the box office and in the boss's office?

Having spent our professional lives crafting and presenting stories that sell—first in the entertainment industry and more recently as corporate consultants—we've realized that all successful stories have five basic components: the *passion* with which the story is told, a *hero* who leads us through the story and allows us to see it through his or her eyes, an *anatagonist* or obstacle that the hero must overcome, a moment of *awareness* that allows the hero to prevail, and the *transformation* in the hero and in the world that naturally results.

These are the five basic elements of every story.

Why five elements and not, say, six or seven? To understand that we have to go back to the dawn of our culture.

Pythagoras was the first great systems thinker in Western culture. He did more than develop that triangle theorem we all had to memorize for our SATs. He pioneered the study of harmonics and created our musical scale. He established the discipline of philosophy, and gave it its name. He founded what was arguably the first modern university. So Pythagoras would be a logical place to start in our study of story. Unfortunately, he left no writing behind. So our story begins with his student, the philosopher and poet Empedocles.

From Empedocles, we first get the concept of the world made up of four elements: Fire, Earth, Air, and Water. A fifth element, implied by his theory but unstated, was added a generation later by Plato and his student Aristotle. Sometimes called "Ether," this fifth element is perhaps more accurately referred to as "Space" because it is the field in which the other elements occur.

Until recently, conventional wisdom viewed Empedocles as a natural philosopher—in essence a protoscientist—primarily trying to describe the material world. More recent scholarship, most preeminently by contemporary philosopher Oscar Ichazo, has shown that the four elements of Empedocles were not solely material but also described inner psychological states. It is in this archetypal psychological sense that Empedocles' elements relate to our understanding of story. They are keys that allow us to see story nonlinearly. Ichazo, whose understanding of the ancient elements is by far the most profound (and whose work has deeply influenced our own), goes so far as to call the elements "ideotropic," meaning that they are ideas that attract our mind to an inner truth in the same way a plant is attracted to the sun.

So how do the five archetypal elements of Empedocles and Plato relate to our five narrative elements? Since story is the carrier of culture, and Empedocles' elements lie at the core of ours, it is not surprising that there is a direct correlation.

Once again, the five-element story model is *passion, hero, antagonist, awareness, and transformation.*

PASSION

Every powerful narrative has passion, the energy that makes you want, even need, to tell it. It is the essential spark, the irreducible cohesive core from which the rest of the story grows. Having it is vital. This corresponds to first of Empedocles' five elements—Fire.

It is passion that ignites the story in the heart of the audience. It is passion that calls the audience's attention to the story in the first place, particularly if the story is aimed at more than one listener.

When an audience first comes to a story, it is composed of separate individuals with differing needs, desires, and distractions. Theater people call a new or difficult audience "cold." They understand that such an audience must be "warmed up" before it can absorb new material.

That is what passion does. It kindles our interests and makes us want to hear more. It unifies us as an audience. And in that unity, which both transcends our self and reinforces it, there is tremendous strength. We turn on the TV every night even when there is nothing really good on just to be part of the story.

The shorter the story, the more powerful the passion must be. A perfect example of a really passionate story well told is the famous "1984" spot that introduced the Macintosh computer to the world. It lasted only sixty seconds. It was only played once on national TV, at the beginning of the third quarter of the 1984 Super Bowl. It almost didn't run at all. People are still talking about it.

At the time the computer industry was in transition and Apple Computer was in big trouble. Apple had been a major player when computers were seen as expensive toys for hobbyists or learning platforms for children. But when corporations began seriously going digital, they naturally turned to a name they had come to trust—IBM. IBM PC computers became "industry standard," with all the purchasing and advertising muscles that implied.

In response, Apple CEO Steve Jobs, one of America's most

passionately committed executives, came up with the Macintosh, a computer that redefined the paradigm. It was easy to use, creative, not corporate, "the computer for the rest of us." It was cutting edge, but unless people found out about it quick, Apple would be buried under an avalanche of IBM sales. Apple needed lots of light and heat, and it needed it fast. The "1984" spot filled the bill.

The sixty-second commercial begins with a line of gray, blank-faced men filling the screen as they march in lockstep down a narrow passage. Orwellian dialogue about "information purification" drones on in the background. Suddenly an athletic young blonde, in red running shorts, carrying a large Olympic-style throwing hammer, runs into frame, pursued by helmeted riot police. The marching men enter a large room where hundreds of others just like them are staring blank-faced at a wall-sized video screen on which the image of Big Brother is pontificating. The blonde runs in, spins around twice, and releases her hammer. It twirls through the air, then smashes into the video screen. The screen explodes in a flash of light that washes over the now startled faces of the prisoners, metaphorically setting them free. The ad's tagline scrolls up: "On January 24 Apple Computer will introduce Macintosh and you'll see why 1984 won't be like 1984."

The result of this ad was explosive. Seven days later there wasn't a Macintosh left unsold on any store shelf in America, and back orders were beginning to stretch out for months. A whole new product area had been created, and the myth that a single ad during the Super Bowl could make or break a corporation had been born.

There are lots of reasons why this commercial was such a successful story. It was written by the legendary adman Lee Clow at the absolute top of his game and filmed by Academy Award–winning director Ridley Scott. It brilliantly piggy-backed its own story on an already culturally accepted myth, the George Orwell novel *1984*, absorbing that novel's energy and making it its own. But at its cohesive core, what made this ad white-hot was Steve Job's passionate belief that a computer was meant to be a tool to set people free.

Real passion, properly focused, makes a story—or a product—impossible to ignore.

HERO

All the passion in the world won't do any good unless you have someplace to put it. That is where the hero comes in. The hero is the second of our story elements and relates to Empedocles' element Earth. The hero grounds the story in our reality. By hero, we don't mean Superman or a grandmother who rushes into a burning building to save a baby, though these are examples of heroes. We mean the character in the story who gives the audience a point of view.

This point of view needs to be substantial enough that the story has "a leg to stand on," but of a scale that allows us to identify with it. The hero is both our surrogate and our guide through the narrative. The hero's vision of the world creates the landscape that the audience enters.

For the audience to identify with the hero's point of view,

they must feel a little piece of themselves in the hero's situation, so part of the hero's function is to create a sense of equality with the audience. We need to feel comfortable walking in the hero's shoes.

In corporate storytelling, this is often the role of the corporate spokesperson. Done well, it can establish a brand. Michael Jordan's "Air Jordan" campaign is a good case in point. When "His Airness" first signed to endorse Nike in 1985, the company was a distant third in the athletic shoe market. By the time Jordan retired, Nike was number one, holding almost 40 percent of the total market, more than twice as much as its closest competitor. Jordan's salary had gone from an initial $2.5 million per year, considered at the time he signed outrageously high, to $20 million a year—and everyone knew it was a bargain.

Michael Jordan is handsome, personable, and talented in a broad number of areas. But what made him really work as the Nike spokesman was that he personified its slogan "Just Do It." To watch Jordan drive toward the hoop, go into the air and soar around a defender, changing direction in mid-leap in a way that made you believe in levitation, was to watch the impossible. He seems to defy the laws of physics. If he can do that, maybe I can do what I've been meaning to do. Get off the couch and get in shape. Go for a run. Play some ball. Try something active. Maybe I can "just do it" too. Of course, first I'll need a good pair of shoes.

By the end of the "Air Jordan" campaign, people had so identified with the Nike story that they weren't just wearing Nike shoes, they were also wearing the Nike trademark swoosh on hats, T-shirts, jackets, you name it, happily making themselves billboards for the Nike brand. Their story and the Nike story had become one and the same.

Having a hero that can bring your audience comfortably into your story is crucial to a successful sales story, particularly when what you are selling isn't a physical product but an abstract concept.

Ronald Reagan was a great storyteller. We're not talking about Ronald Reagan the president, but about Ronald Reagan the Warner Brothers–trained movie star, ex-president of the Screen Actors Guild, and former host of *General Electric Theater*. As the "great communicator," he knew the importance of heroes. He understood that with the right hero, people would see even dry and technical facts from a personal viewpoint. So during his State of the Union addresses, when he got to a point that might be abstract or an issue that might be divisive, he would point up to the Congressional Gallery and there, posed and waiting, was an "American Hero" who personified the point Reagan was trying to make. Reagan controlled the national debate by using heroes to define the territory it would cover. We understood his stories because we knew his heroes—they were the same as us.

ANTAGONIST

Problems are like water—without them a story dries up and blows away. Antagonists, and the conflict they represent for the hero, are the beating heart at the center of the story. By antagonist we mean the obstacle the hero must overcome. The antagonist doesn't have to be a person—if the hero is struggling to climb Mount Everest, the antagonist might be the mountain itself—but there has to be an antagonist. If the hero faces no obstacles, there really is no story. If there were no defenders, Michael Jordan jumping up and putting the ball in the hoop wouldn't be much of a story at all. But since there were—the Detroit Pistons had been double-teaming Jordan all night long, we were in the final seconds of game six of the Eastern Conference playoffs, and the Chicago Bulls were down by only one as Jordan started his drive down the lane—it was really big news and an unforgettable moment.

The passion of the contest catches our attention, but it is the emotions released by the hero's victory that lock the story in our memory.

Stories often personify conflict in a villain, someone we love to hate. Two-time Academy Award–winner William Goldman says there are only three questions you need to answer to start a good screenplay: "Who is your hero? What does he want? Who the hell is keeping him from getting it?" This is how Goldman defines conflict.

The Dalai Lama, who won the Nobel Peace Prize for his understanding of how to deal with international conflict, put it in more general terms: "Each one of us has an innate desire to seek happiness and overcome suffering." He also said, "Your enemies are your best teachers."

Great stories mirror this reality. Seeking happiness is our motivation. Overcoming suffering is doing battle with our internal and external antagonists. Instinctively, humans are interested in how others deal with their problems. Funneling this curiosity into the narrative is what releases the emotions that wrap around the facts and create the story.

Research, including high-tech real-time brain scans, is now showing that emotions, triggered in the limbic area of the brain—also known as the mammalian brain—lock a story in memory.

This is particularly important in a sales story. It's no good selling the board of directors on your idea if they forget all about it when you walk out the door. We'll be talking about the connection between emotions, conflict, and memory in a later chapter, but the antagonist provides more than just a memory hook.

Where would Hamlet be without Claudius, Luke Sky-walker without Darth Vader, the Road Runner without Wile E. Coyote? It is the antagonist that makes the hero's actions meaningful. The same is true for corporate stories.

Roberto Goizueta, the former CEO of Coca-Cola, consciously used this principle to revitalize Coke when it was in danger of becoming moribund in the 1990s. By directly attacking his main rival, Pepsi, Goizueta rallied his own troops and triggered what were known at the time as the Cola Wars. In an interview with Jack Welch for *Fortune* magazine, Goizueta suggested that a company that did not have a natural enemy should go out and find one. When asked why, he replied, "Because it is the only way to have a war."

And for Coke, the Cola Wars worked. For a time the conflict between the two corporate giants, Coke and Pepsi, released tremendous advertising and marketing energy as they struggled for market dominance around the world. New sales techniques were discovered and perfected, new markets opened, lots of money was made all around. But in the end, when neither side could gain a decisive advantage, the story became boring. So be sure the antagonist you use in your story is one your hero can overcome. The dragon is there to be slain, not to become a pest.

Of course, not every story has a happy ending, and there is a real moral danger in creating villains. Living in Germany in the aftermath of World War I was frightening and brutal. Adolf Hitler wrapped that fact in the powerful emotions of paranoia and anti-Semitism. How passionately he conveyed those emotions can be seen in the surviving films of his speeches. The story he told—that the Jews were responsible—compelled the German people to take actions that transformed the world into a living hell. Storytelling is innate in human beings, but it is in some respects a value-free process.

Fortunately, there is a fail-safe. Those stories that produce destructive and negative actions tend to cannibalize the people who tell them. They rapidly eliminate themselves from the cultural dialogue. If you want your story to survive and have a long and profitable life, be sure not to demonize your antagonist. The function of the villain is not to create conflict, but to clarify it so that it can be overcome.

AWARENESS

So what allows the hero to prevail? How is the villain defeated? In a really bad story it might be a moment of dumb luck, or a character we've never met before who shows up with the combination to the locked safe, but in a good story—the type you'll be telling—it is a moment of awareness.

Awareness corresponds to Air. It is literally the inspiration the hero has that lets him, or her, see the problem for what it is and take the right action. Emotions make the hero want to move. But if he or she doesn't make the right move, the effort will be wasted.

In detective films, this element is highlighted. The moment the hero, having carefully pieced together all the clues, suddenly gets it is often marked with a musical throb, a close-up, or even a brief flashback. However it is done we know that he knows who the killer is! We see it in the look in his eyes. If it is an older film, like the classic *The Thin Man*, he might invite all the other characters into the dining room and lay it out for them. In screenwriter terms, he would "make a meal of it."

In real life, these moments are often very brief, almost like flashes of lightning, and it is sometimes easy to leave them out of a story, but putting them in is crucial.

Legend has it that Thomas J. Watson, the founder of IBM, had such a moment of awareness that changed everything. Locked in a struggle with Olivetti for control of the typewriter market, he suddenly realized something about IBM that he had never seen before. In a flash of inspiration he saw that

IBM wasn't in the typewriter and adding machine business; it was in the information processing business. That discovery made all the difference. IBM moved into computers, and the rest is history.

There is something magical about these "aha" moments. Like air, they are almost impossible to get your fingers around. In fact, though the story of Watson's moment of inspiration is widely told and believed—no one we have discussed this with doubts that it happened—it has been very difficult for us to run down exactly when and where it happened. Once you have heard the story, it seems so self-evident and obvious that you just accept it. Knowing about that moment of inspiration makes IBM's corporate story—otherwise one of a relentless, repetitive rise to power—much more exciting. In the history of IBM it is like a breath of fresh air.

When you are looking for these moments of awareness in your story, one clue is that they are quite often triggered by the smallest detail.

Adam Kahane, formerly a scenario planner for Royal Dutch Shell, tells the story of a meeting he had as part of the Visión Guatemala team, a group that was working to find a way out of the seemingly endless cycle of violence and revenge that had marked the Guatemalan civil war, one of Central America's longest and bloodiest. His team had gotten representatives of many of the stakeholders—the army, the rebels, politicians, priests, villagers—together to talk. For days they had heard each other out, describing acts of unbearable cruelty committed by both sides. Things seemed to be going nowhere.

Then one politician described going to the exhumation of a mass grave at the site of a particularly brutal massacre. When the bodies were removed, this man noticed that there were still tiny little bones left at the bottom of the pit. He asked the forensic scientist doing the work if those were the bones of animals, perhaps monkeys that were somehow buried as well.

"No," he was told, "many of the women killed that day were pregnant. Those are the bones of their unborn children."

A quiet fell over the room. Deep and profound, it lasted not for seconds, but for minutes. And when the discussion began again, everything had changed. The image of those tiny little bones had made everyone aware just how horrible the civil war—a war they had all lived through and participated in—had really been. Afterward the participants in the conference said it was that moment that had made all the difference. It was at the moment that they really decided that things had to change.

Awareness is not always easy or comfortable, but if you want your stories to make a difference, it always has to be there.

TRANSFORMATION

Transformation is the element that needs the least explanation because it is the natural result of a well-told story. If you've taken care of the other elements, it just happens. Our heroes take action to overcome their problems, and they and the world around them changes. This of course relates to the element of Space. Change is the playing field on which stories are told.

At the beginning of *The Iliad,* Achilles is in a snit, refusing his duties to his comrades in arms, but ends the story defeating his enemy, Hector, and honoring his fallen foe in death. Hamlet dithers in a world of moral ambiguity, but in the end takes actions that remove a great evil from the heart of his kingdom. Luke Skywalker accepts the reality of the Force and gives the Republic new hope.

Successful stories don't have to have a happy ending—the last scene of *Hamlet* is hardly a laugh riot—but they all involve change.

In sales stories, you often don't give transformation a lot of thought because the change you want to produce is a given. You want to transform your listener from the owner of a five-year-old Yugo to the proud possessor of a spanking-new Ford. You want to transform your client from an apartment dweller into someone who has invested in a white-picket-fenced piece of the American Dream. You put your attention in other elements. Getting them motivated to stop kicking tires and actually buy. Getting them to see the house the same way you do, as perfect for them. The story you tell them might do it, or it might not, but you know where you are headed right from the start.

But there is one type of business story where transformation *is* the story. These are leadership stories.

In his classic book *On Leadership,* John W. Gardner makes

the point that the modern organization, whether it is political or corporate, depends on leadership from the factory floor to the highest executive suite. In this fluid, information-intensive environment, who ends up being the leaders? Usually it's the people who can effectively tell the right story—a story that harnesses the group's energy to deal with a common problem.

Let's face it—leading is a lot more fun than following. Even if you never want to be a CEO or to change the world, you do want to have control over your own work and your own ideas. Ultimately, that is what the power of story can give you.

That is the transformation we want this book to produce. *Elements of Persuasion* can help you be that leader. It will help you use stories to build morale, strengthen teamwork, and define problems, then step back from them so that you and your coworkers can discover original and effective solutions. Then it will help you sell those solutions so they actually happen.

In the following chapters, we are going to talk about each of the five elements of successful storytelling in a lot more detail. So, what do you say? You want to hear a few good stories? It won't take long. And we promise you it will be worth your while.

We will be including exercises that will help you polish your storytelling skills. They won't be time consuming, difficult, or embarrassing. Here is the first one. It is something you'll be doing anyway.

Tomorrow, tell three stories. Any three stories. You'll tell many more than that in a normal day, but this time tell them while being consciously aware of the five elements each story contains. Either as you are telling them, or right afterward, run through these questions like a mental checklist:

Passion: Why did I tell that story? What makes me care about it? Did I make my audience care?

Hero: Who was the story about? Did the person I was telling seem to accept the hero's point of view?

Antagonist: What problem was the hero confronting, and how did telling that story make me and my listener feel?

Awareness: What did my hero learn in the story? What did I add to the cold facts to make it sparkle?

Transformation: What changed in the story?

Now listen to three stories others tell you, using the same questions. Why are they telling me this story? Who is the story really about? And so on.

It's an easy exercise. No one need know you are doing it (unless you want to make that a story of your own), and you'll be surprised at how quickly you get the hang of it. It will definitely help you remember the stories of others, and you might even begin to collect them. As any good salesman knows, collecting other people's stories can be a very valuable habit to have.

CHAPTER TWO

Fire in the Belly—
Personal Persuasion

Dave Austgen is the type of client we love working with. Dave is General Manager, Technology and Operations, of Shell Hydrogen, a division of Shell Oil—the Fortune 50 company. He left a position in the chemicals division—one of Shell's core businesses and the conventional career path to continued corporate promotion—to move to one of Shell's newest divisions and focus on alternative fuels. He came to our consulting firm, FirstVoice, which specializes in corporate and executive communication strategies, with a problem. He was scheduled to give a twenty-minute talk at a government conference on alternative energy policy. His audience would consist of potential partners, competitors, government regulatory agencies, and environmental NGOs. He would be presenting Shell's plans in a paper titled "Developing the Hydrogen Economy Infrastructure." Some in his audience were technical experts; others knew almost nothing about this particular subject. An engineer with a PhD in chemical engineering, he was concerned his material might prove too dry and technical, and with a title like that we agreed it didn't seem like a barn-burner. He told us his corporate mandate was to use this conference to convert competitors into collaborators in what could prove to be a multibillion-dollar investment in R & D.

Dave is a nice guy who speaks with the refined twang that you associate with the Texas oil patch. He is clearly very, very smart and carries himself with the physical assurance that comes from being a successful player of the corporate game. We were curious, so we asked, "Why did you leave the most stable and secure division of your corporation—petrochemicals—and move to an alternative fuel division that is still experimental?" We wanted him to tell us his story. And he did.

He told us about the places he had visited in his life, places of great natural beauty that he feared would not be there for his children because of global warming. He told us of walking through the mists of the Amazon rain forest, of standing on an overlook at Glacier National Park in Montana, of watching the birds rise up into the sunset over the Florida Keys. And he told us that he honestly felt that the project he was involved with—the development of a hydrogen alternative to fossil fuels—might be a big part of the solution. He told us he wanted to make a difference. And he told us he was a businessman. He was convinced there was big money—big money even by oil industry standards—to be made by being part of the solution rather than part of the problem.

It didn't take him long to tell us. No more than a minute or two, but it made a lasting impression. When he was finished we knew that though his talk might indeed need to be highly technical, it would be a home run. Dave had the one thing that every storyteller—and that is what public speaking always is—must have before all else. Dave had *passion*.

Passion is the first of our five elements. Without it you can't get started. You can barely get out of bed really, let alone inspire a roomful of strangers. It is the fire in your belly that makes you need to tell that story, and that makes everyone else need to listen. It is the "why" of the story—why you are telling it, why we are drawn to listen.

Finding it, in yourself and in your presentations, is absolutely essential to how business is done today. The days of the lifetime corporate paycheck are over. Even in Japan they are no longer handing out pensions in return for being a nameless, faceless cog in the corporate machine. The "company man" is out; the "corporate entrepreneur"—often grouped with others in small boutique-style teams to maintain competitive mobility—is coming on strong. We may all want security and a steady paycheck, but what we are actively looking for is the next big thing. We will know it when we see it. If we don't see it first, we will know when someone else does. We will see it on his face, in the slight gleam in his eyes, in the passion in his voice that can barely be contained. Allan Weber and Bill Taylor, founders of the magazine *Fast Company,* captured this spirit in their slogan—"All business is personal." Whether you are working your way up through the mental minefield of a modern corporation, burning the midnight oil as part of a creative team, or coming in early to make cold calls looking for new clients, if you are not personally committed and passionately involved, why should anyone else care?

Getting other people to care about what you care about is what this book is all about.

The first thing that any of us needs to do if we want our ideas to prevail in the marketplace is to speak up. Unfortunately, in survey after survey, public speaking is ranked number one among commonly held fears—far above fear of accidents, disease, or terrorist attack. Which means, as Jerry Seinfeld says, "Given the choice between giving a eulogy at a funeral, or being in the coffin, most people would rather be dead." Public speaking is scary.

And the public doesn't have to be that large. Speaking up in a corporate boardroom is often as stressful as talking to a large group, and asking your boss one-on-one for a raise is guaranteed to spike anyone's blood pressure. Luckily, the first minute or so of your talk is the hardest. After that it usually gets easier. It is more than just making the right first impression—though that is very much part of it, and we'll go into how to do just that. It is also getting over the hurdle of one hundred thousand years of evolution.

For most of our time on this planet humans have lived in small tribes, and meeting members of other tribes was at best dangerous. You certainly didn't go alone. The habit we have of shaking hands—and showing that we are unarmed—is a remnant of those days. So the first thing we tell our clients who are going to give a public presentation—or make an important sales pitch—is that the fear they feel is absolutely natural. We all feel it, and it is among the most intense fears we ever experience.

A few years ago the U.S. Army did a research project on what made the best soldiers. The researchers determined that it wasn't lack of fear they were looking for. Fear, and the adrenaline reaction that goes with it, greatly sharpens the senses and is a positive survival trait. What they wanted were people who could quickly go into the heightened awareness fear brings, and then, just as quickly, shake it off and do what had to be done. In combat, that's a matter of life and death. But what could they use to test people to find those who got frightened but didn't freeze? Video games are great simulations for some things, but they don't touch our deepest fears.

The Army shrinks came up with a simple test. They ordered the soldiers they were testing to give a speech on a subject they were only marginally familiar with to a roomful of strangers and monitored the reaction. For everyone, heart rate shot up, blood pressure spiked, there was an increase in "dry mouth" and rapid, shallow breathing—all the expected stress reactions. What the psychiatrists were looking for were the soldiers whose physiology quickly returned to normal after the initial shock. Those were the ones who were ready to lead. Our point is this: you don't have to go to Iraq to feel like your life is on the line. Sometimes just thinking about walking in front of a roomful of strangers is enough.

And there is no getting used to it. Professional actors experience that same physical reaction. One British medical study ranks stress levels of professional actors on opening night as "equivalent to a car-accident victim." If you feel like you've been hit by a truck, you're not alone. Even Sir Laurence Olivier, the greatest actor of his generation, struggled with stage fright his entire career, to the extent that he would ask other actors not to look him in the eyes when he was on stage. He felt too vulnerable and close to panic.

As we tell our corporate clients, everyone is frightened. The question is, what are you going to do about it? We suggest you do what you do best. What all human beings do best. Tell a story, the more personal and passionate the better.

So we suggested that Dave open up his talk to the energy conference by telling them what he has told us—about his travels, his kids, his dreams for the future, his vision of making a difference. Dave wasn't embarrassed to go into all that (briefly, of course), but he was concerned. The farther up the corporate food chain you go, the more corporate-speak and the "royal we" worm their way into your language, and the more risk averse your culture is. Being a senior manager at Shell is pretty thin air. Dave was worried that by talking about his feelings rather than repeating the company line he would be leaving himself open for sniping. And he was right. He was taking a real risk. It was a risk that paid off (how well it paid off we will get to in a moment), but it took courage. Like we said, Dave is the type of client we love to work with.

Starting your presentation with a personal story—how personal is a matter of your comfort level—offers two immediate advantages.

First, stories, particularly our own stories, are very easy to remember, and given the pressure of the moment, why would you want to make things hard for yourself? The last thing you want to do is freeze right at the start. The glazed deer-in-the-headlight look that comes over speakers as they struggle to remember their first line—or when they hide their eyes as they read off their script, then furtively look up—is a bad first impression that is very hard to get past. Come across as natural and relaxed by doing what you naturally do: tell me a story. It doesn't have to be long. If it is your story, not one you had written for you, the audience hears that authenticity in your voice. Human beings are very good at picking up exactly that type of cue at first meeting. Evolution, remember. Humans who couldn't do that have long ago been eliminated from the gene pool. As worried as you are about the audience, they are just as cautious about you. So win them over by being real and relaxed.

Second, stories quickly allow you to do the two things that all the research shows are most important for increasing your "likability" in the first sixty seconds of your presentation: share something personal, and show the audience that you are talking to them, not simply giving a canned speech or sales pitch. If you think about it, this is exactly what the classic comedy act opening does. The comic strides onstage at the club and says, "Hi, I just got back from LA, and I've got to tell you those freeways are something else. Now, I'm from Brooklyn [something personal] . . . anyone else here from Brooklyn? [The act opens out to include the audience as someone calls back and answers yes.] "Yeah, where? . . . Really, I know that neighborhood. Wild place. So, like I said, I'm not at all used to freeways . . ." By being personal and open to the audience, the comedian makes us think, "Hey, I like this guy." And it works even if we are aware of how carefully planned that interaction is. Of course, if the comic isn't really from Brooklyn, he or she had better be a very good actor.

One reason jokes so often bomb when they are used to open up a corporate speech, getting at best polite and nervous chuckles, is that professional comedians use jokes to reveal something personal about themselves—the more real and personal the revelations, the funnier the jokes. Too often corporate speakers hide behind their jokes, using them to cover nervousness or deflect potential opposition to what is coming later in the speech. Maybe the most embarrassing is the corporate CEO whose patter is written by a gag writer and designed to make him seem like just one of the guys. The material might work great in a club, and read very funny on the page, but at the beginning of a presentation to shareholders it comes over as stale and prepackaged, exactly the reverse of the desired impression. This is a pity, because all the boss had to do to be one of the guys is tell us a story about his family, or his house, or his day at the office. Or something he has just seen that makes him know the company is on the right track. The sort of things we all share in common. Compared with even the best prepackaged joke, a good story is easier to remember, easier to deliver (as the old show business saying goes, "Dying is easy, comedy is hard"), and much, much more effective.

Former Speaker of the House Tip O'Neill built his career on knowing how to open a speech this way. An extremely skillful ward-level politician from Boston, O'Neill's first position in national politics was as head of the Democratic Congressional Campaign Committee. It was a job that had him traveling to all the congressional districts in the United States. In each he would give a short speech, then do a little fund-raising. He made it a habit to always ask his hosts to take him someplace that was unique in the community on the afternoon before his talk. Truman's house in Missouri. A Civil War battlefield in Georgia. Where wasn't important. What mattered was that people knew it was local and unique. Then Tip would start his speech by talking about his trip to the local landmark, and what it had meant to him, and how seeing it had made him feel. It was a personal moment, and clearly it wasn't called in. It connected him to the people he was talking to. People liked that. They liked it so much that when he got around to requesting funds, they took out their checkbooks and Tip went on to become one of the most effective Speakers of the House in recent memory.

So there were good reasons why Dave should take the risk of starting his energy conference talk with a story. It was a risk, but the risk was one more reason to do it. Because people love to watch other people take a risk and win. We root for the man on the flying trapeze. We cheer for the NASCAR driver who weaves his way through burning tires and twisted metal to head for the checkered flag. If there weren't risk involved it wouldn't be interesting. And we are wishing them well. When people go out on a limb, we don't want to see it cut off.

A few years ago, Marshall Goldsmith was the keynote speaker at a conference on how corporations could hold on to their best talent. It was a weekend conference, and the first day was dull to the point of disaster. That night the conference sponsor sat down nervously with Marshall and, over what Marshall now calls "perhaps a few too many martinis," came up with a plan to save the event.

The next day, Marshall's address to the audience of mostly corporate HR executives opened with a serious question: "Just how far are you willing to go to hold on to your highest-performing talent? What are you willing to do—not say, but actually do—to stay competitive?" For instance, should they allow them not to wear a jacket to corporate meetings even if it violates a dress policy? At this point, Marshall took off his jacket. And what about a tie? Can you let go of the tie? Marshall could; he took off his tie and threw it aside as he continued to talk about some of the common problems creative types have in corporate culture. Well, in for a penny in for a pound—what about that starched white shirt? Let's get rid of it, too. At this point the audience was on the edge of their seats. Shoes, socks . . . they are only thinking one thing. When will he stop? How far will he go? Is he going to take off his pants? That was what they were looking for. But what they were listening to was his talk. Underneath everything else, he was posing a serious challenge—is your corporation so hidebound by corporate traditions that it is strangling its own future? And he was underlining one of his key points—actions talk louder than words.

Now, before anyone runs off and commits sexual harassment around the watercooler in the name of promoting a good idea, we should stress that Marshall pulled this off for three reasons. One, what he was doing wasn't just to shock; it was connected to the theme of his talk. Two, as a master corporate coach, Marshall is extremely skilled at picking up the physical cues that signal other people's comfort level, and as he was doing his thing, he had his inner radar turned up full blast. As intent as his audience was on asking, "How far is he going to go?" he was asking himself, "How far can I go?" If at any moment he heard the audience laughter begin to shift from genuine amusement and take on a nervous edge, he was prepared to stop. So everyone in the room was rooting for the same thing—for him to get right up to the edge but not to cross over. If you play with fire, you have to be careful not to get burned. Marshall did a masterful job of testing the limit and stepping back, to rousing applause. And third, as well as being the world's highest-paid executive coach, Marshall is also not a bad stripper. If at any moment he had become embarrassed and crossed out of his own comfort zone, the whole house of cards would have crumbled. It was his passionate commitment to what he was saying that allowed him to stay focused on his message and hold it all together. The audience loved it. This happened five years ago, and people are still talking about that speech.

So—people love to root for people who take a risk and win as long as they are passionately committed to taking it. Just ask Bill Clinton.

There is probably no more risky action in modern American politics than Clinton's January 1998 White House press conference where he wagged his finger at the camera, looked us all straight in the eye, and said emphatically, "I did not have sexual relations with that woman . . . Miss Lewinsky."

In all but the most technical sense, he was flat-out lying. In doing so he was risking a president's most precious possession—the trust of the American people. Now, we are not defending what he did, and the politics of the situation are open to debate, but not by us, because we are not in the politics business. We are in the communication business. So what fascinates us is how this simple statement, which very quickly was clearly contradicted by the facts—including the famous DNA on the blue dress—actually strengthened Clinton's support. He went up in the polls and he stayed up in the polls, and the more he was attacked, the more he went up in the polls. The more that clip was shown on the news, the more the country polarized with the majority rallying around him. It was against the laws of political gravity. It was like watching someone levitate. As Republican commentators constantly reminded us, the world is not supposed to work like that. It just wasn't logical.

But neither are people's primary motivations. The sorts of motivations that make people decide to support your idea or ignore it. Clinton might not have had truth on his side, but he had passion. In both senses of the word—and that semantic link is more than just coincidental, because there is, as Marshall's performance also demonstrated, something distinctly (though not necessarily overtly) sexual about passion. Passionate love brings us all into being and binds together our most intimate relationships. Passionate hatreds fuel feuds and prejudices down through generations. It is tricky stuff, this passion, but our most respected heroes, from Prometheus on down, are the ones who can play with fire and still come out winners.

"Winners" is the key word. So what can you do to make sure that when you take the risk of giving a public talk that breaks the mold and actually puts what you care about on the line, you win?

Well, first, realize that having people angry with you is not losing—at least, not totally. Totally losing is having people not care enough about what you are saying to pay attention and stay awake. Committing to your passion is usually enough to deal with that, so you are already halfway home. Second, realize you are in a fight. If you weren't, you wouldn't need to persuade the audience; they would already be on your side and you could probably just send them a memo. Since you are in a fight, and losing is going to take the bread out of the mouths of your babies (even if those babies haven't arrived yet, trust us, Grasshopper, they will), you should do your homework and study war from the masters. The two masters we recommend are Sun-tzu's *The Art of War* and Miyamoto Musashi's *The Book of Five Rings,* also called *Writings on the Five Element*s.

Sun-tzu's *The Art of War*, written during the classical period of the Chou dynasty (551 to 249 BC), is the world's first great manual on warfare, and is still used by the finest militaries, including our own Marine Corps, as well as by most forward-thinking strategic business planners. Musashi's *The Book of Five Rings* is the work of Japan's foremost swordsman and was penned in 1643 in the prefecture of Kyushu while the famous samurai was meditating in a cave. Don't let the meditation aspect fool you. It is a marvelously bloodthirsty account of how to lock swords with any enemy and walk away with your head and both arms still attached to your body. For years it has been used as primary text for training executives in Japan's zaibatsu corporate culture. As the global economy expands and Asian markets continue to grow exponentially, learning from our potential competitors is just plain smart. These books have a lot to teach us about war as a struggle of ideas.

Sun-tzu's classic begins, "War is a matter of vital importance to the State; the province of life or death; the road to survival or ruin . . . Therefore appraise it in terms of the five fundamental elements . . . The first of these factors is moral influence; the second weather; the third terrain; the fourth command; and the fifth doctrine."

Substitute your company name for "State" and you get the idea. Sun-tzu's five elements and our five elements are roughly analogous. What he calls moral influence, we refer to as passion. So before you walk into a room and present your new idea, ask yourself a few fundamental questions to make sure the force is with you. Do you really care about what you are about to say? Is it true? Leave lying to the professionals. If you can't find anything true about it, pick another idea to talk about. Sun-tzu further defines moral force as what makes people follow their leaders "even unto death." Your idea doesn't need lukewarm supporters. You are looking for people as willing to take a risk for it as you are. For that, it needs to be hot.

In terms of meetings, what Sun-tzu calls weather, we call timing. The energy of a business meeting in the morning is totally different from the energy of the same sort of meeting right after lunch, when everyone is full and just a little lazy, and totally different again from a meeting just before closing, when the caffeine has worn off and most people's creative energy has been spent. So when is your meeting? Best to set it for early in the morning, but you may not be able to control the time. You can, however, modify your presentation to fit the slot you have been given.

The morning is bright, sharp, and cutting, and you can take the time to tell the details that substantiate your plan. After lunch, you need to refocus your audience's energy. People are always a little sluggish after a meal, and there is a natural energy dip between two and four (which is why some countries have siestas), so be aware that you are going to have to work to keep your audience on task. Keep it light and nimble. No part of your presentation should be longer than five minutes, and if you are working in a team, hand off the speaking role often. If you are planning a PowerPoint presentation, for God's sake don't dim the lights. Before closing, people's energy is spent. Don't expect them to decide; work to make them remember. Strip your presentation to the bone and go for a quick, strong close. Your goal is to have them thinking about your idea that night.

By terrain, we mean the actual physical location you will be in. If you are presenting to a group, arrive early. Lord Nelson—the British navy's most successful admiral and the hero of Trafalgar—said he owed all of his success to his habit of arriving fifteen minutes early for every engagement. That is a habit you need to develop. It will give you time to get to know your equipment. Make sure your PowerPoint runs and the sound system is properly adjusted. Try out the space you will be using. If you must give your presentation seated, sit in your seat and get comfortable. Make sure you have a chair that doesn't squeak when you shift your weight. If you can make your speech standing, do it that way, but be sure not to get trapped behind a podium. The eye loves movement, particularly movement toward or away from us. Think of all those great movie shots when the hero rides toward us seemingly forever, or the beautiful girl runs toward us in slow motion. On a stage, movement from side to side comes across as pacing, and it works only if you are actively thinking of an answer. Otherwise, avoid it. Here is a quick trick. When you are discussing the future, take a step forward and toward the audience. When you mention the past, take a step back. And when you are in the here and now, be centered and still.

When Sun-tzu says command, he means the general, and that means you. The most important quality of a general is courage. Aristotle defined courage not as the absence of fear, but as the correct balance between timidity and overconfidence. The best field general we've seen is Joe Montana, former quarterback of the San Francisco 49ers. He is on the motivational speaking circuit, and if you get a chance to see him you should take it. He has the ability to effortlessly command the audience's attention and totally lives up to his nickname of "Joe Cool." He tells a story of his throwing the game-winning touchdown during Super Bowl XXIII that is so elegant and graceful it is not to be missed. We'd tell it to you, but really, this one you have to see for yourself. The story is in the way he holds his body, the way he cocks his arm back to throw the imaginary pass, the intensity that comes into his eyes, and the calmness that fills his voice. By the way, going to see really good public speakers speak is a great way to become one. Make a point of doing that.

Sun-tzu's final element is doctrine, though some translations refer to it as politics. This is your game plan. The spine of your speech. Rehearse it out loud. You don't need to know your speech word for word—in fact, if you do, it tends to come across as stilted—but you need to be totally familiar with the sequence so that if something unexpected happens, and it always does—the mike cuts off, a waiter drops a plate, or your PowerPoint blows a fuse—it doesn't shake you up. Don't memorize your speech, just say it over and over a few times. Reading silently is not the same thing at all. Our rule of thumb is to do it five times, and at least once or twice before a live audience—even your cat counts, but your buddies are better. If it is twenty minutes long or more, tell them you'll buy them a beer afterward—or, better yet, tell them you will return the favor the next time they need a sounding board. Then ask them what worked and what didn't. You'll have learned a lot already just by paying attention to their reactions. Rehearsing in front of an audience, even an audience of one, is indispensable and increases your confidence. Resist the temptation to talk about your speech. Don't tell them what you are going to say—say it. Your talk needs to come trippingly off your tongue. Some things that work on the written page just won't come out of your mouth easily. Cut them and find another way to say it that feels comfortable and pleasing to your own ear. It needs to sound right.

Finally, know what you want your audience to do once you stop speaking. You aren't there just for the applause. You have invested a lot of time and energy successfully getting them on your side. Now tell them specifically what you want them to do. Keep it simple, keep it clear, and keep it doable.

Sun-tzu is for strategy. He is your classic big-picture guy. Musashi, the samurai, is up close and personal. He is all about delivering the killing blow.

Miyamoto Musashi is a Japanese cultural icon. His life has been the subject of numerous novels and movies, including the classic Samurai Trilogy starring Toshiro Mifune. Muhashi was an orphan from a samurai family who killed his first man in a sword duel at the age of thirteen, then spent the next thirty years traveling through Japan challenging the best warriors to personal combat, all with the goal of perfecting his art. He never lost. Along the way he became a master of Japanese brush painting and calligraphy, and his artwork graces some of the world's finest galleries. He saw that the pen—at least the Japanese ink brush that is its equivalent—is not just mightier than the sword, but is a natural extension of it. A dedicated Buddhist, at the end of a life that had taken him from poverty to the most refined levels of Japanese society, he retired to a cave and contemplated what he had learned and what he had to teach. The result was *The Book of Five Rings*.

This book is extremely practical in terms of how to wield a sword, control your opponent's lines of attack, and use timing and rhythm to your advantage—all important points to remember in public presentations—but at the heart of his matchless technique was what Musashi called *hitotuse no uchi*— "winning with a single strike." As he says, "Gain the capacity to win with certainty by keeping in mind the single strike. This is the way of victory in all combat. Exercise well."

In modern kendo fencing, when such a blow is delivered, the contest is over and the winner declared. It has been described as a blow that "resounds in the heart and mind of the one that receives it and also in the mind of the one who delivers it." It is the quintessential story. A fact—the blow—wrapped in the pure, spontaneous emotion that allowed you to deliver it— transforms you into a winner. It is a moment of pure passion.

William Safire, former speechwriter for Richard Nixon and the *New York Times* columnist responsible for keeping the world grammatically correct, certainly knows what makes a good speech. He has written enough of them. And he says that at the center of every great political speech is a single extremely memorable line that contains in simple language everything the speech is working to convey. Who would remember Kennedy's inaugural without "Ask not what your country can do for you—ask what you can do for your country" or Roosevelt's first inaugural without "the only thing we have to fear is fear itself"? And Ronald Reagan's simple command, "Mr. Gorbachev, tear down this wall!" still rings through history. They are in language form what Musashi meant by the single strike. They contain the essence of the whole speech. They are the spark that made the speaker need to speak in the first place, and the torch that gets passed on. The idea they contain spreads because it is the nature of fire. It's contagious.

We always recommend to our clients that once they have their speech ready, they work on getting it down to a single, easy to remember sentence. You may never deliver that sentence as such, but having it ready and keeping it constantly in the back of your mind is your most important edge.

So after we worked with Dave Austgen on his speech for the energy conference, making sure it contained all five of our essential story elements (passion, hero, antagonist, awareness, transformation), we worked with him on his core sentence. Because he did know and really care about what he was talking about, it was easy for him to come up with. "As an alternative to fossil fuels, Hydrogen Cell Vehicles are possible and very profitable, and they are the right thing to do right now." He never said it in his talk—he never had to—but if he had been confronted from the audience, he was ready with the killing blow.

How did the talk go for Dave? Remember Dave's mandate. Shell wanted to find potential partners in a massive R & D process. Well, at the end of his twenty-minute presentation, Dave was approached by four major players in the energy field (and when Shell says major, they really mean *major*) who wanted to explore the possibility of strategic partnerships. As a result, Dave's project for building a hydrogen economy infrastructure, which we think really might be a big part of solving the problem of global warming, is moving full speed ahead. And it happened because Dave was passionate enough about what he had to say to take a risk on using the power of story.

CHAPTER THREE

Brush Fires—Motivating the Masses

So, you more or less know what to do if you want to walk into a room and sell people who need widgets the widgets they need. As long as both you and they care about widgets, it's a done deal. If they don't care yet, by the end of this book you will know how to get them to care. But what if you personally can't make those visits? How do you motivate your sales force to go out and do it for you? Or what if you are trying to sell millions of widgets to millions of people in millions of living rooms all over the country? If you are part of a high-end design shop, personal persuasion may be the only skill set you really need, but the people you are selling to—the corporations that depend on tapping into mass markets—will still need your help to broaden their appeal. Even the most creative of the creative entrepreneurs needs to know how to take it to another level. Luckily, one of the advantages of storytelling as communications strategy is that it is easily scalable.

A good story plays as well on TV as it does whispered to a guy in the back of a union meeting hall. It's as powerful in the powder room as it is in the boardroom. People love a good story. We can't get enough of them. And a good story is infectious. It spreads like wildfire.

One reason is that a good story always has an element of surprise. In fact, Jerome Bruner, the cognitive psychologist we've mentioned before, postulates that stories always arise out of the unexpected. If your partner arrives home from work every day at 6:00, and he doesn't show up by 6:15, your brain, want it or not, is busy creating stories to explain the situation. He (or she) is heroically struggling to get through freeway traffic, or her evil boss is making her work late, or he remembered today is a special day and has stopped to get flowers. Whatever story you are imagining, the storytelling process itself is allowing you to take an event that you can't control—your partner isn't here—and turning it into a narrative you can. In doing so it is letting you try out possible responses you will use in the near future. If the freeway story is the one that proves true, you will be ready with a kind word and maybe a martini. If it is the flower shop, then you are ready with "Oh, you shouldn't have" and a vase.

The element of surprise that lies at the heart of a good story is one reason they are so fascinating. People love puzzles. Engage my curiosity and you have my total attention. It is also one reason that some of the shortest and most infectious stories—the ones that spread quickest—are jokes that play with surprise.

Take Henny Youngman's classic borscht belt one-liner, "Take my wife . . . please!" It is just four words long, and once you've heard him tell it, you can't forget it. It works so well because his delivery makes us think that he is doing a common comedy segue, "Take my wife . . . ," then he shifts gears and surprises us with the plaintive " . . . please!" An emotional plea to be free from her nagging. That moment of surprise engages our own inner storytelling response, and we immediately fantasize reasons why he might want to get rid of her. Nothing elaborate. Just a few fleeting mental images. But by triggering that reaction he has taken us from passive listeners to active participants in his act. So we do what active participants at a comedy club are supposed to do: we laugh. We indicate that we got the joke, that we figured out the puzzle. Because the surprise and the solution come so quickly together, the psychic result is particularly pleasant. In the age of the Internet, a good joke can circle the world in less than twenty-four hours. And a great joke stays funny for years, adapting to changing conditions while the punch line stays the same.

This ability of stories to deal with the unexpected and actively engage us in finding solutions is one reason that the most successful large corporations harness stories as primary motivators. This is particularly important for those companies whose mass market is on the edge of becoming commoditized. The high-end hotel business is just such a situation.

When you rent a hotel room, you are basically getting the same thing whether you are at a Motel 6 or at the Ritz-Carlton. You are renting four walls, a bed, and a night's sleep. The reason you pay so much more for the Ritz is a long list of intangibles, most of which come down to one thing—the Ritz treats you right. And no one knows how to treat you righter. The Ritz-Carlton chain is the only hotel group that has won the U.S. Department of Commerce's prestigious Malcolm Baldrige award—and the Ritz has won it twice. It does it by making you feel like a member of the family. Like the bar in *Cheers,* the Ritz seems a place where "Everybody knows your name."

One reason is that the Ritz chain has by far the most sophisticated database in the industry. If you order your martini shaken, not stirred, in New York (and this is the last time we'll mention martinis, we promise), when you check into the Ritz in Beijing, the bartender there already knows how you like it. Getting a staff of over thirty thousand employees at sixty-three hotels on five continents to pick up on those sorts of subtle details, care enough about them to note them down, and then remember to look at the list later is no easy trick. To get everyone on the same page, Ritz uses what Sue Stephenson, the senior VP of human resources, calls "WOW Stories."

Three times a week, the daily "Line Up" (the team meetings that occur before a shift change) is dedicated to the reading of WOW Stories. These are stories in which an employee somewhere in the world went above and beyond the call of duty in providing for a guest's special needs. WOW Stories are submitted to the main office, the best are chosen, and then these are sent back out in the daily briefing packet, so that on any given Monday, Wednesday, and Friday the same story is being read and talked about all over the world. The stories are chosen to reflect corporate themes—for example, anticipating the unexpected—and these themes then can be discussed in a natural and fluid way. Instead of coming across as a corporate directive about how you should behave, it comes across as positive reinforcement for how people just like you are already behaving.

There is a lot of prestige in the Ritz corporate culture from having your story chosen. The stories are submitted by management, but most often involve the actions of the primary sales force—the people who are actually making one-on-one contact with the customers. If your WOW Story is chosen to be read, there is a small—$100—financial reward, but it is mostly about bragging rights. Your peers all over the world will know what a good job you are doing. After a WOW Story is read and discussed, other stories that come from the local hotel naturally come to mind. It is like any college dorm bull session. It gravitates to "can you top that," and so it sparks a virtuous cycle of storytelling that rewards and reinforces the behavior that makes the Ritz the Ritz.

Once we heard about how they were using stories, we had to go check it out. We hadn't been in the lobby of the Marina del Rey Ritz-Carlton more than three minutes—in fact, we had barely had time to say "WOW Stories"—before we began to hear about Fran Adams's story. It was chosen as one of the top ten WOW Stories of 2004 (there is a competition), and everyone at the hotel still takes great pride in repeating it. It is worth repeating here.

Like a lot of good stories, it starts on a dark and windy night. In this case, a blustery February when the downstairs bar that Fran tends was largely deserted. "The only one in the room was an older gentleman, the sort of executive that has been drinking the same scotch for the last fifty years." A young, good-looking couple—we'll call them Dick and Jane—came in dressed in luau shirts despite the weather and ordered mai tais. They seemed a little morose, but Fran is the sort of bartender who can get anyone to open up, and soon they told their story. Dick and Jane had just been married. They had always planned to honeymoon at the Ritz-Carlton in Kapalua, Hawaii. In fact, they had a reservation already booked for six months in the future, but Dick had just been diagnosed with cancer—a particularly nasty form of Hodgkin's lymphoma—so they pushed the date forward and were in LA for chemotherapy. This might be as close to Hawaii as they ever got, so they were bravely trying to make the most of it. When Fran tells the story, at this point her eyes take on that slightly stunned look that comes to cancer patients as they struggle to find the right balance between hope and denial. Obviously, the couple's story touched her deeply.

Fran got someone to cover the bar and sprang into action. She found Don Quimby, the manager on duty, and together they went to the banquet hall prop room and collected anything that reminded them of Hawaii—a fishing net, a collection of starfish and seashells, a poster of Hawaiian hula dancers at a luau—and quickly gave the couple's room a makeover.

They even filled a cooler with sand and stuck in a sign that read "Dick and Jane's Private Beach." Then Don found an electronic key from the Ritz at Kapalua that a previous guest had left behind by mistake and reprogrammed it so it worked on Dick and Jane's room door. Don put on a Hawaiian shirt and went out to deliver this new key to them. He led them to their "new Hawaiian Honeymoon Suite," where a complimentary bottle of champagne was waiting. And for the next three days the staff of the hotel did everything it could think of to make the couple feel like they were on the Hawaiian honeymoon of a lifetime.

Now, as a marketing ploy this is brilliant. It is the sort of thing that starts an avalanche of word of mouth. They had given Dick and Jane just the kind of honeymoon story they want people thinking about when they hear the name "Ritz-Carlton." All of Dick and Jane's friends were going to ask how things went in LA. When they heard this story, they were going to want to stay at the Ritz themselves, and they were going to pass the story along to their friends, and so on and so on. But what makes this story even more remarkable is that it doesn't come from some marketing maven at headquarters; it came up from the grassroots interactions that are the heart of the hotel business.

When Fran's story was chosen as a WOW Story, she received calls and e-mails from peers all over the world, many of whom she had worked with in the past, telling her how great the story had made them feel and congratulating her on a job well done. After it was chosen as one of the top WOW Stories of the year, she received a letter from Simon Cooper, the chain's president and CEO, praising her dedication and letting her know how much he personally appreciated her story. She said that what meant the most to her was "that letter wasn't on his corporate letterhead. It was on his personal stationery." Even when a story is used at the corporate level, it is always heard as very personal.

Now, Fran is obviously an exceptional employee (though for the Ritz she is more the norm than you might think), and holding on to employees like her and keeping them motivated is one of the goals of any good HR program, so we should mention that after telling us this story Fran paused and added, "You know, my family often asks me why I still hold on to this job. I never get holidays off; those are our busiest times, so I can't celebrate with everyone else. And I could work anyplace. But I tell them, where else could I be that I could do so much good for people. And where else would it be so appreciated. I mean . . . this job is addictive."

The storytelling culture at Ritz doesn't end, or even begin, with WOW Stories. The corporation takes its motto "Ladies and gentlemen serving ladies and gentlemen" very seriously. To get a job you need to go through three interviews. The first is just a get-to-know-you talk in which the interviewer makes it clear that working for a hotel chain is very hard, demanding work, and nothing like the experience of staying at a luxury hotel. It is the second interview that is most crucial. To develop the approximately fifty questions that are asked during this interview, Ritz-Carlton partnered with Talent Plus. They took several hundred high-performing employees across the full range of hotel positions and looked for the personality traits that separated them from an equal number of more marginal employees in the same jobs. Then they came up with questions to find out whether the interviewee had the desired personality traits.

Karrin McCarron, the head of HR at the Marina del Rey Ritz, is one of the people trained to give and understand that interview. It can be tricky, because the answer to some of those questions is pretty obvious. Hotels are a service industry. The correct answer to "Do you like to help people?" is—duh—a no-brainer. So for forty-five of those fifty-five questions there is a follow-up. If you answer yes, Karrin will ask, "You say you like to help people. Could you give me an example?" If you were just giving the expected response because you knew what was expected, you tend to answer in a generality: "Well, all the time, really. It is just what I like to do." But if it really is what you like to do, you will answer with a specific story, because one just pops into your mind: "Well, my Mom is getting older, and I like to go by and help her with the cleaning. When we are in the kitchen we get a chance to talk. The other day . . ."

As Karrin puts it, "At Ritz, we say the story is proof of action."

In our storytelling terms, the interviewee's story demonstrates an emotional commitment to the trait Ritz is looking to hire. Because stories are facts wrapped in emotions, if the fact is real and connected to the emotional quality Ritz is looking for, it will automatically create a story that will immediately come to mind. Facts, emotions, awareness—the three keys to correctly using story in business.

Being a good storyteller, and a good story listener, are skills that take practice, but they very rapidly move through a corporate culture and become positive habits. On the day we went to the Line Up for the day staff, Karrin, who normally begins each day's discussion, didn't have a WOW Story to read. The meeting was mostly focused on how to smooth out the difficulties caused by a remodeling project in what it calls "the heart of the house" (the behind-the-scenes areas that guests rarely see). These difficulties are the sort of low-grade stressors that make a business feel just not quite right to customers, who never know why they decided to go someplace else with their cash the next time. Karrin, who had been away for a week taking some personal time, began by saying that she appreciated the good wishes she had received on coming back. Her father had taken a bad fall while repairing his roof and broken both legs. The surgery had gone well—her being there had been important for both of them—but his life was going to have to change. Luckily, he had good friends who rallied around him. They got together and built an access ramp to his front porch so being in a wheelchair for the coming months won't make him a prisoner in his own home. And seeing that he had so many good friends willing to come together to help was the best medicine her dad could have had.

From there it was an effortless transition to the corporate point—difficulties with the remodeling don't have to set us against one another. If we all work together they will actually make us a better team. Everyone in the room nodded; they got the point. At the end of the meeting, many people came up to Karrin with brief stories about how something similar had happened to them or their parents. This story worked so well as a motivator because it was true and heartfelt. But it came across as simple and authentic, rather than as some corporate parable from on high, because it is just the sort of story that people at Ritz tell each other, and are listening for, all the time. It is the type of story that knits communities together, and it is one reason that Ritz enjoys one of the lowest levels of employee turnover in its industry. The company spends a lot of time and money finding and training the right people. Keeping them is a priority.

So, stories are good to motivate a sales force that is relatively compact and that meets routinely to share them. But do they work equally well when your sales force is totally diverse, spread over many continents, and needs to be largely self-directed and self-sufficient? In that situation, they might be the only thing that really does work. Take the example of Mary Kay, Inc.

Mary Kay's story is one we like to tell because it is a story that begins with a story. In 1963, Mary Kay Wagner, having been involved in direct sales from the 1930s on, got tired of being passed over for promotion by what she considered less-qualified males (the Equal Rights Amendment was still years in the future). She decided to retire and write a book telling other women how to supplement their incomes by going into sales. In telling her story she realized that she had actually stumbled onto a great business model. So she scraped together $5,000, dumped her idea for the book, and started a corporation instead. Today Mary Kay, Inc. has over a million sales representatives—which it calls "beauty consultants"—in thirty-five countries with a yearly income of well over $2 billion. Mary Kay has over four hundred thousand sales reps in China alone! And that is why *you* should be interested in this story. While such corporate icons as GE and General Motors are still struggling to get a toehold in the China market, Mary Kay, with its down-home emphasis on story, is already in and just keeps growing. And that despite the fact that the Communist government changed the rules and made Mary Kay's traditional distribution technique—door-to-door direct sales—illegal. But because what links the Mary Kay sales force is a web of shared stories and corporate myths, told at giant sales conventions in Houston, and over brewing teapots in villages all across China, what could have been a stopper was barely a bump in the road for this company. As Bruner pointed out, stories are a reaction to the unexpected, so a story based on corporate strategy is extremely flexible; and because storytelling is inherent to the human condition, it is transcultural. The stories may change; the storytelling doesn't.

Liang Yan doesn't go door-to-door anymore. Instead, she works a sidewalk in Wangfujing, Beijing's always-packed shopping district. When she spots a potential female client, she invites the woman around the corner and up to a small second-floor room. There, over a pink table, she gives her new friend a full beauty makeover. It takes about two hours. And they do what women anywhere in the world do in a beauty parlor: they talk, gossip, and tell stories. But Liang's stories aren't just selling the products. They are selling her passion as a member of the Mary Kay team. She is selling a career path.

Mary Kay uses a classic vertical marketing structure. Sales reps move up the pyramid by getting others to become sales reps under them. Along the way they get a small piece of their new recruits' profits in return for providing the distribution connection, product knowledge, and emotional support. Of the three, it is the emotional support that is most binding.

Every year toward the end of July, more than fifty thousand of Mary Kay's most successful distributors descend on Dallas and take over the Convention Center. They are easy to spot. Most are dressed in Mary Kay's distinctive pink. And they are all smiling. They have come together to honor the year's new national sales directors, those women who, through patience, hard work, and dedication, have made it to the top of their corporate pyramid. At a mass meeting more like a tent revival than a conventional sales meeting, the year's winners will receive the ultimate Mary Kay status symbol—a garish pink Cadillac.

These meetings in Dallas always start with a prayer session following the Mary Kay model for a balanced life of "God first, family second, and career third." (In China this is translated as "Faith first," but the idea stays the same.) Then, as each of the new directors is awarded their car, they step up and tell what is always an inspirational story—that ability to inspire is a big reason they made it up the pyramid to become director—as the crowd cheers. It is an evangelical moment—pure passion focused on one person's success. You can see it on the faces of the women telling their stories, and in the ecstatic expressions in the audience.

Ironically, it is just this communal passion that led the Chinese government to move against direct marketers (not just Mary Kay, but Amway and others) in the first place, calling them "weird cults, triads, and superstitious groups." What allowed Mary Kay to so quickly adapt was its core corporate story.

A woman, a worker, feels oppressed. She realizes that the power to change things is in her own hands, and so she turns to other women like herself, not to overthrow the system, but to make it more efficient and responsive at a grassroots level. A Mary Kay director doesn't succeed by defeating the competition; she succeeds by fostering positive traits in those below her. She succeeds by becoming the model worker. It is a story that has to warm the hearts of even the most hardened Maoist. As Liang Yan says, "I can make more money in a month than my whole family can make in a year of hard work. Welcome to the place where we enrich women's lives."

So passionate storytelling is a key to corporate motivation and success. Why? Because human beings are wired that way. And no one knows it better than the people who sell cars.

Hormones and their neurotransmitter cousins are the chemicals that control much of how we react to the stories that confront us every day. Adrenaline triggers our fight-or-flight response. Insulin makes us feel safe and secure (which is one reason chocolate makes us feel loved and appreciated), thyroxine sharpens awareness. The most powerful hormones in humans are the sex hormones—testosterone and estrogen. These determine whether we are male or female. Every human has both; it is the mix that matters. And it is at this level that car companies make their most powerful pitch.

Buying a car is a big deal. It is the second-largest purchase most consumers will ever make. And unless your car just went belly-up on the freeway, it is a purchase that is easy to delay. So getting people to actually sign on the dotted line is in some sense the ultimate test of a salesman's motivational art. It begins with knowing who you are selling the car to.

From the drawing board on up, there are two kinds of cars, just like there are two kinds of buyers. There are male cars, testosterone cars that are marketed with ads that feature smoking tires, roaring engines, and hands working the gearshift knob. Cars like a red Ferrari Testarossa. These are the cars young men buy so they can go out cruising and hopefully get lucky. Their ads feature elements that are completely familiar to the reptilian brain—quick movement down serpentine roads, splashing through puddles, or scooting across the desert floor, as a tiny, id-like voice whispers in our ears, "Zoom-zoom."

Then there are the female cars, the cars soccer moms buy to keep their kids safe to and from school. The cars designed to protect the results of all that late-night cruising. These car ads feature children climbing in and out at the curb and always putting on their seat belts, and brakes that always stop in the nick of time. Volvo in particular built its whole brand image around this type of car, but SUVs, which are demonstrably less safe than your average sedan, learned to subtly exploit this market as well.

G. Clotaire Rapaille, a cultural anthropologist whose work many of the car companies use to help them reach their potential customers at the deepest level, explains that it isn't safety per se that matters, but rather the feeling of safety. "The number one feeling [people want] is that everything around you should be round and soft and give." Not, we note, unlike a mother's breasts when she holds you safe. So there needs to be lots of air bags. "Then there is the notion that you need to be up high. That's a contradiction because the people who buy SUVs know at a conscious level that if you are high there is more of a chance of a rollover. But . . . they feel bigger and taller and safer. You feel secure because you are higher and dominate." Going further in his analysis, he adds, "What was the key element of safety when you were a child? It was when your mother held you up high in her arms and fed you. There was warm liquid. That is why cup holders are absolutely crucial to safety. If there is a car without cup holders, it is not safe. It is amazing that intelligent, educated women will look at a car and the first thing she will look at is how many cup holders it has." Amazing maybe, but if you are planning on selling cars, it shouldn't be surprising. That is one story detail your design team needs to know and address. To a large extent American car companies are remarkably skillful at understanding who they are talking to and how to reach them at this deep level.

Which is why William Clay Ford Jr.'s fall from grace is such a classically tragic tale. If you think that you can one day get high enough in your company hierarchy that you won't have to be constantly tailoring your story lines to motivate the people below you, think again. If anyone was in that position, it was Bill Ford. His name wasn't simply on the door. It is dead center of the logo attached to every car that Ford makes. The great-grandson of the company's legendary founder, Henry Ford, and Firestone founder Harvey S. Firestone, Bill was to the manor born. His family is by far the largest stockholder in the company. He grew up being treated like royalty in Dearborn, the corporate home. But he didn't get the CEO job through personal connections. He spent his entire adult life training for it, starting on the factory floor cleaning the windows of cars just rolling off the assembly line, then moving into the company's finance division—Ford's traditional training ground for future top executives—and spending time as a midlevel executive in product development. By 2000 he was in charge of Ford's heavy-truck division, one of the global corporation's perennially successful profit centers. He knew the company, he knew the people who owned it, he knew his job.

And to a large extent he knew the future. He recognized that the record profits Ford was making in the late nineties were heavily dependent on cheap gasoline and truck-based SUVs, and that gas prices couldn't stay low forever. A bit of a New Age businessman who got his MBA at MIT, he was passionately committed to building new "green machines"— hybrid vehicles that could get great gas mileage without sacrificing performance or safety. And he made this personal commitment in 2000, long enough before the market "suddenly" shifted toward fuel efficiency (when gasoline predict-ably reached three bucks a gallon) that Ford should have been perfectly positioned to move and dominate the market. But it wasn't. Toyota, with its trendy-looking Prius, was. When the dust settled in 2006, Toyota had for the first time replaced Ford as the number three selling brand in America (it had long since been number one in the world). Bill Ford had the right idea at the right time. What he couldn't do was sell it to his own people.

If you are going to use story as a motivator, you have to be careful that what turns you on in a business situation is the same thing that turns on your audience. That is particularly true if you are trying to reach a mass audience. The workforce at Ford is massive, over seventy thousand in factories on five continents. To a large extent they are passionately linked to the company, and there is a strong sense of family. Many factory workers are third- and even fourth-generation employees. Bill Ford is a classic example. And they love cars. Talk to any of the company's designers or executives and not long into the conversation you will hear about the car they have in their garage that they tinker with on weekends. These guys are motor heads. So when Bill Ford came out and was widely quoted in the press saying that his would be the generation that would end Ford's dependence on the internal combustion engine, it wasn't a turn-on; it was a massive turnoff. The people working for him didn't want to be part of the death of something they loved; they wanted to be still burning rubber and roaring top down into the sunset as far into the future as their imaginations could reach. So his employees did what employees always do when you turn them off—they began to drag their feet. Instead of happily solving problems, they began just as happily creating them. His design teams fell behind schedule. The engineers didn't quite come up with the technical solutions they should have. So when Ford's hybrid SUV—the Escape—finally did come out, it was an overpriced, underpowered also-ran. Company stock tanked. To try to save the situation, Bill had to step aside for a new CEO imported from the aircraft industry. Whether that will be enough to stop the tide of red ink is at this point an open question.

Bill Ford had made the classic CEO mistake. He thought what turned him on (being a responsible corporate citizen in an age of global warming) would turn everyone on. But it didn't. It did just the opposite. He had the facts right, but they were wrapped in all the wrong emotions.

Being a Monday-morning quarterback is easy, but imagine what would have happened if instead of trying to reach out to his team across New Age corporate responsibility, Bill Ford had reached out across old-line family values. He was in a unique position to talk about faith in Ford as something that was passed down from father to son. And from the factory floor on up his company is very tuned to that sort of story. In fact, the problem that is most weighing on Ford is a transgenerational problem: how to provide health and pension benefits to retired workers. One reason that the union is so adamant that there won't be any rollbacks in health care is that the current membership are the sons and daughters of those retired workers. They aren't about to let their parents get screwed over. If their parents don't get the medicines they need, they hear about it immediately. For Ford, family is a powerful motivator.

So what would have happened if instead of announcing the death of the internal combustion engine Bill Ford had stood up and said, "A hundred years from now, I want my children and your children to be driving down computerized highways totally safely at two hundred miles an hour in a gleaming new Ford. Working together, we can do that. But the world is running out of oil, so we are going to have to find some other way to power those big engines. But, hey, we are the sons and daughters of the people who invented the assembly line, for gosh sakes. Inspiration is in our genes. We can carry that torch forward and make Ford number one as we roar into the bright future, not just because we are talented and committed, though all of us are, but because we stand on the shoulders of giants!"

Would that story line have worked better? It couldn't have worked worse.

Now compare Bill Ford's story with that of Peter Schultz, the first American executive to take over as CEO at Porsche AG. We'll let him tell it.

"Making decisions is easy, but getting things done or implementing decisions is difficult . . . As new president at Porsche, I attended all our races. I was there to observe and hold the flag. My first race was Sebring USA. It was very exciting to watch these monster Porsche 935s with seven hundred horsepower move around the track. Porsche won that race.

"When I got to corporate headquarters in Germany, I called a meeting. I was higher than a kite after Sebring and I knew there was low morale at the company. I asked what is the most important race of the year. It was the 24 Hours of Le Mans, and that was just sixty-two days away. I asked if we would win." Here his voice shifts into a light German accent as he continues. "Well, you see Mr. Schultz, you don't understand. We cannot win. We have entered two 924 Porsche turbos. They are production cars racing against full racecars. There is no chance of winning. Perhaps we can win best in class.

"One of the most important functions of a CEO is to make it clear what in the Sam Hell we are all doing around here. So I told them we were all going to meet again the next morning at 10:00 AM and I wanted them to tell me one of two things. Either how we were going to win that race, or what they were going to be doing at whatever new job they were planning to look for. As long as I was president, Porsche was never going to a race that it didn't intend to win.

"The next day was a magic moment. There was electricity in the room. Morale was high." His voice shifts into an accent again, this time filled with a playful lilt. "Well, Mr. Schultz, there is a way. We can take the engines out of the 924s and connect them to the transmissions from the 917s, and if we . . ."

It wasn't just the attitude of the people in that room that had changed. Word of the change of corporate direction raced through Porsche. Peter Schultz continues: "Two days later I got a phone call from Jacky Ickx. He was one of the finest drivers in the world, and he was in retirement. He said he had just heard a rumor that Porsche intended to win at Le Mans. If it were true, he would like to come out of retirement and drive for us. Suddenly, a number of other top drivers wanted to drive for us as well. We won that race. And we went on winning for the seven years I was head of Porsche."

In story terms, what Peter Schultz did was connect the new passion he had felt at Sebring—the visceral, almost sexual excitement that comes when you are down in the pits breathing a heady mix of smoking tires and half-burned hydrocarbons—with the simmering frustration that his best designers felt when the previous management had refused to commit to the one thing they really cared about: winning races. Winning races was why they had come to work for Porsche in the first place. Porsche's racing pedigree is why it sells the cars it sells, and why its owners are so fiercely loyal. What Schultz did at that meeting was like lighting a match and dropping it into a gas tank. In this case the explosion was totally positive. As he puts it, "I discovered an important management secret. If you want to attract the best people to do what they do best, you don't do that with money. You have got to have an exciting project. People want to be part of a winner. If you want to attract and hold on to the best people, you need to make them feel that they are part of something larger than any one of them."

So how do you do that? Well, you tell them your story and you listen to theirs, and you make sure that what connects them isn't just good thinking, but is also a passionate commitment to your common goal. You bring people together and get them hot for your ideas, so hot that those ideas become their own. From both a creative and a management viewpoint, that is the ultimate turn-on.

So, to sum up. Storytelling as a corporate communication strategy has a lot going for it.

1. Stories are extremely contagious. They can spread very rapidly through even the largest corporation in part because people love to gossip. Telling a good story is fun. Making your story that story is not really all that difficult. This book is going to keep telling you exactly how.

2. Storytelling is scalable. Whether you are a small creative team coming together on a short-term design project or a part of a large corporation setting multiyear goals, finding the right story is the key to success.

3. Stories bring people together and build real team loyalty. That is important if you are in a close-knit team that meets together often (like the Line Ups at the Ritz), and it can be even more important if members of your sales team are spread across the globe, like the beauty consultants at Mary Kay.

4. Because, as Jerome Bruner points out, stories are based on a natural human response to the unex-

pected; story-based strategies are extremely flexible and adaptive. When the Communist hierarchy in China made door-to-door sales illegal, the Mary Kay myth allowed that company to quickly regroup, adjust sales technique, and win approval. But the story has to be honestly told and needs to connect to a commonly held core passion.

5. Passion is the first of our five elements, and it is what drives your story forward. It is operating even at a hormonal level. It is the vitality that is at the cohesive center of your story. If you can't get people to connect to your story at that level, you are telling the wrong story.

CHAPTER FOUR

Everyone Is a Hero— How Stories Build Trust

Warren Buffett is our hero. Not because he is the richest man in America—his close friend Bill Gates holds that honor. Not because of the uncanny ability to look into the future and pick stock winners that earned him the nickname "the Oracle of Omaha"—he is the first to say he remains America's premier investor not by predicting the future but by accurately assessing the value of a company in the very solid here and now. And though he has been a constant voice for reforms in corporate governance that help the average investor (and who of us with a 401(k) can't get behind that), we aren't rallying around his flag for that reason either. So what does make him our hero?

Well, as businessmen, and particularly as communications consultants, we need to keep an eye on the big picture to fit our client's story into the overall story stew that is our culture. Corporate culture is highly competitive. We need to know who is winning and why. The score is kept on Wall Street. But neither of us is very good with numbers—in fact, quite the opposite. So we need someone who can take all that raw data and put it in a human context that even we can understand, absorb, and use.

Whoever can do that is our hero. All we really need is a few wise words to set us in the right direction. We are like tourists in a strange land, and we are looking for that scenic overlook, the place where we can pull off the road for a moment and get our bearings. All we need is the right point of view. After that, the rest falls into place.

If you want to understand the American economy as it moves into a new and increasingly global century, Warren Buffett's point of view is the clearest and cleanest. And as the over fourteen thousand shareholders in his company, Berkshire Hathaway, that crowd into the arena in Omaha for his annual meeting will attest, Buffett is very generous about sharing it.

These events are more like down-home county fairs than your typical proxy-filled corporate snooze-a-thons. Most of Berkshire's subsidiary companies (like GEICO) have booths set up selling their products at substantial shareholder discounts. There is even a not-to-be-missed barbecue. The main event is when Buffett, and his investing sidekick Charlie Munger, take center stage for six hours and answer any and all questions from the audience. These sessions are so open, honest, and informative that many parents have ponied up the almost $100,000 that a share of Berkshire Hathaway costs just so their kids can attend these meetings and see how the world of business works when it is done right.

Comparing his annual meetings to those of other companies, Buffett says, "Many annual meetings are a waste of time, both for shareholders and for management. Sometimes that is true because management is reluctant to open up on matters of business substance. More often a nonproductive session is the fault of shareholder participants who are more concerned about their own moment onstage than they are about the affairs of the corporation. . . . Under such circumstances, the quality of the meeting deteriorates from year to year as the antics of those interested in themselves discourage attendance by those interested in the business.

"Berkshire meetings are a different story. The number of shareholders attending grows a bit each year and we have yet to experience a silly question or ego-inspired commentary."

So as the ringmaster of this circus, how has Buffett managed to pull off such a long string of meetings that never go sour?

By very carefully listening to the stories contained in the questions he is being asked. When he responds, he responds with great good humor and not only with facts, but also with the emotions that surround them and make them matter. He puts things in a context that can be easily understood. He can do this because he is not trying to impress anyone. He isn't trying to get you to see things his way and prove that he is right. He is just opening up his considerable store of experience and intellect and sharing it. That way, when you do naturally see things his way, the awareness arrives with a sense of discovery. It is your sense of discovery that matters. You trust that discovery because you are the one who made it. You trust him for helping.

That is what heroes do. They open up complex stories, welcome you in, and make you feel at home. They do it by letting you see the world through the hero's eyes. The fact that Warren Buffett is a seriously kick-ass good writer (he won the 2005 National Commission on Writing Award for being "a unique leader who many in business and industry see as a rarity because of his proven ability in explaining complex thoughts with just the right words") is just icing on the cake. But it is no accident that *our* hero would be a great storyteller.

As we mentioned before, *hero* is the second of our five story elements, and is related to the ancient Greek element Earth. It has a lot to do with defining your territory and markets. That is one reason that our oldest cultural heroes were kings and the founders of empires. The hero is the story's point of view personified, and our guide through it. Every story needs a hero. Creating (or more often *finding*) the right hero is one of the most important tasks you, as a corporate storyteller, need to do. In most stories, choosing your hero is the first decision you will make.

If I am telling you the story of the stock market, I know what you're passionate about—making money. That is what makes the story hot. And if I don't deal with that—or you're not interested—we won't have much of a conversation. But past those first thirty seconds when we establish we both want the same thing (to get rich), I need to find a way to make my story connect with your world at a broader level. I need to find a common denominator, a place that you and I can both equally understand and get behind.

The key is finding that sense of equality with your listener—always difficult in business relationships, where we tend to divide things into winners and losers. Buffett is famous for maintaining equality with the shareholders of Berkshire Hathaway, whom he prefers to talk of as his "partners." This is one reason why, despite being one of the wealthiest men in the world, he keeps his salary at a very modest $100,000. As he said in one annual report to shareholders, "Charlie and I can't promise you results. But we can guarantee that your financial fortunes will move in lockstep with ours. We have no interest in large salaries or options or other means of gaining an 'edge' over you. We want to make money only when our partners do and in exactly the same proportion. Moreover, when I do something dumb, I want you to be able to derive some solace from the fact than my financial suffering is proportional to yours."

We trust a guy who says that, means it, and backs it up with years of actions. Who wouldn't? And because we trust him, we're not constantly shifting capital in and out of his stock (Berkshire is your classic buy and hold bargain), so Buffett doesn't have to worry about his own stock price and can focus on doing his job. This is one more reason for you to find the right hero for your story. Having the right hero in your story builds trust and lets your boss or your client relax and stop micromanaging, so that *you* can do your best work.

Warren Buffett may seem to be all things for all investors, but we didn't choose him for our hero by looking for the lowest common denominator. That sort of race to the bottom is almost always a loser. We found Buffett by looking for someone who seemed to know what he was doing, clearly enjoyed it, and was willing to talk about it in a language we could understand. That Buffett represents the *highest* common denominator is one of the great characteristics of a hero. Heroes naturally bring out the best in themselves, the listener, and the story.

We trust Buffett as a hero in part because he is a complex and interesting person. We don't want a cardboard hero. No one does. We want someone with a unified point of view (otherwise the story gets confusing), but someone who sees that the world around him is constantly changing, so the view through his eyes is always shifting as well. If it isn't, there is something wrong with the picture.

We instinctively don't trust one-dimensional heroes, and when you are crafting your own story, avoid them like the plague. Winning the audience's trust is what the hero is all about—if they don't trust you they aren't going to give you their money, no matter how great your new idea might be, and that is why we're talking, right?

There are a wide range of hero types, and cultural bias plays into how you are going to construct your story, particularly if you are going after international markets, but all heroes do four crucial things.

1. They make us feel a sense of equality. If we don't feel that link, we reject them. Looking at the world through the hero's eyes is a very intimate relationship. If we don't synchronize and link up at an almost physical level with the hero, it won't work. It requires trust. Warren Buffett is a good example of how you can earn that trust in the business world.

2. They stand their ground. Heroes control some territory. Physical, emotional, intellectual, or spiritual. They have turf and they have an edge. They control something of value. They are the Prince of Denmark, or have just invented the ultimate search engine, or are the owner of three magic beans. Whatever they control, the important thing is that they have worth. That isn't an accident. As Mr. Buffett (and other corporate spokesmen) clearly show, the right corporate hero is the ultimate value-added for any company. The connection between wealth and hero is a by-product of evolution. Land was the original measure of a person's wealth. More cattle, more status. More status, more children, and a bigger effect on the overall gene pool. Things may have become a little more abstract in the last twenty-five thousand years, but the connection of heroes to wealth remains rock solid. Just think of Michael Jordan's salary. That glitter of gold (in his case from the six championship rings on his fingers) helps hold our attention.

3. Heroes never lose their capacity to surprise. Because they are just like us, with lots of complexity, they

remain fascinating. It is hard for a storyteller to create that sort of complexity out of thin air, which is why we recommend you *find* a real live hero to put in the center of your story. It is easy to do. Just look around. There are heroes everywhere. When your hero does deliver a surprise, it can't come out of left field. The spark of awareness that is going to come at the end of our story (you remember, the "aha" moment that allows the hero to triumph and brings such satisfaction) is prepared for in the nature of the hero you have chosen. If Luke Skywalker hadn't started out the story wanting to become a Jedi Knight, his hearing "Trust the Force, Luke" wouldn't have much effect on either him or on us.

4. Heroes act as good guys. It is the hero's commitment to what the ancient Greeks referred to simply as "the Good" that makes their winning so enjoyable. That is why Babe Ruth's visiting kids in the hospital and promising to hit them home runs, and then, against all odds, delivering, is such a part of his heroic myth. Heroes don't need superpowers; in fact, they tend to work against them (if Superman weren't vulnerable to kryptonite and misunderstood by his girlfriend we would rapidly lose interest), but they do have to be good guys. A little rough around the edges maybe—a "Dirty Harry" sneer is certainly allowed—but corporate heroes are *always* good guys. Leave your angst-ridden antihero in the foreign film bin where he belongs.

Buffett demonstrated all of these heroic traits when, on June 26, 2006, he walked into the Reading Room of the New York Public Library just off Times Square and in front of Web cameras set up by his friend Bill Gates, who was sitting at the table next to him, publicly committed giving the bulk of his private fortune ($38 billion—that's right, *billion*) to helping solve the pressing health problems of the third world. That there was wealth involved goes without saying. Though he is famous for structuring Berkshire Hathaway so that it is very easy and painless for his shareholders to make charitable contributions, he is also known for not playing the CEO charity game in which corporate money is used to make the head honcho look good in the papers. So his sudden announcement of his own charitable contribution caught Wall Street by surprise and produced a tsunami of positive buzz for Berkshire (not his intent, but good heroes just can't help but increase corporate value). It is his commitment to maintaining his equality—his sense of being one of us—even as he performed this unique act of largesse that makes the most lasting impression. He could have chosen any venue for the broadcast. He chose the New York Public Library, a place any citizen can use and feel welcomed. He could have set up his own foundation—the Buffett Foundation—so that every check came with a little "look at me" reminder of who you should thank, but instead he put all that giving under someone else's name. Those checks will read "The Gates Foundation." And he gave the money to someone *he* trusts, the only person who could put more of his own money into the pile than him because, as he explained, "Just because I'm good at making money doesn't mean I'm good at giving it away." Like Dirty Harry once said, "A man should know his limits." Like we said, Warren Buffett is our hero.

Putting the CEO out front as the corporate spokesman (or being willing to step out front yourself and be the hero if that is what it takes) doesn't always work, but when it does, it works gangbusters. We don't know why it works so well for selling chickens.

Perdue Farms, one of the nation's largest poultry providers, began as a backyard business. Back in the 1940s, Frank Perdue and his father raised chickens for eggs at the family farm in Salisbury, Maryland. In the 1960s, Frank took over the business and shifted from selling eggs to selling the chickens themselves. It wasn't long before he decided to cut out the middleman and started selling his birds directly to grocery chains, not to commodity providers. He began selling them from an ice bucket in the back of his car. Then he did what corporate heroes always do—he listened carefully to his customers and his point-of-sales representatives. He went on the road, traveling to thirty-one states and talking to butchers at the large chains. He carefully listened to what they told him and found there were twenty-five things people wanted in their chickens.

People preferred birds whose skin had a healthy golden color, so he added marigold seeds to his feed mix to give his chickens that hue. People didn't like those annoying little pinfeathers that used to be on the wings, so he figured out a way to burn the pinfeathers off before final packaging. Customers wanted more breast meat, so he developed a new breed of chicken, the Perdue breed, which had more of the tender white meat customers craved. He had built a better mousetrap, but to get the world to beat a path to his door, he still had to go out and tell them about it.

Once again he cut out the middleman, becoming one of the first CEOs to go on the tube and personally sell his product directly into our living rooms. Between 1971 and 1990, he appeared in over two hundred ads, all done by the hot and nimble ad firm Scali, McCabe, Sloves. Frank was not by any stretch of the imagination movie-star handsome, though his beak nose, bald head, and puffy eyes did give him a slightly birdlike look that didn't hurt. What made the ads work was the way he talked about what he knew about best: his chickens. He totally believed that he sold superior chickens, and like Buffett explaining the stock market, he wasn't shy about telling us why. In his early ads, Perdue appeared in a white butcher's smock, and though later he was often wearing the neatly tailored suit he had earned as tycoon (by the late 1980s, he was one of America's four hundred richest men), you always got the sense that he wasn't far off the slaughterhouse floor, where he made sure things were done right.

If you look at those early ads, his obsession with the details of poultry farming is fascinating. He made it clear his chickens were treated right all the way to the market. They were never frozen. In one spot, he even drives a nail into a board with a competitor's frozen chicken as the "hammer" to show how untender and unappetizing freezing makes meat. He stressed that his birds were fed "only the finest grains," given only "pure well water to drink," and told us why that mattered. "Chickens are what they eat. If you want to eat as good as my chicken . . . then eat my chickens."

People all over the country did. Perdue Poultry was a highly successful single-family farming operation making $58 million in 1971. Then Frank's first ad as corporate hero hit the air and things rapidly changed. Soon he controlled an empire employing over twenty thousand associates and partners at seventy-five hundred independent family farms generating profits of over $2.8 billion. Along the way, he stuck with one ad house and one slogan—a slogan we had come to trust: "It takes a tough man to make a tender chicken."

The ads worked because we instinctively knew what he was saying was true, but most viewers never knew how true or how tough a man it took. As Perdue expanded his processing operation into southern states, he ran into the inevitable labor disputes. Meatpacking is dangerous work. By definition, there is already blood on the floor. Labor disputes in that industry can get dangerous real quick. In 1980, Local 117 of the United Food and Commercial Workers Union began an eighteen-month campaign to organize his plant in Accomac, Virginia. Tensions escalated. The union brought in its big guns, even having Rosa Parks and Rev. Jesse Jackson talk to the largely black workforce. Frank fought back, increasing his already famously workaholic schedule so that he spent more time on the factory floor with the guys wielding the knives and delivering the goods. He showed by example (and that is another characteristic of a good hero) that he worked just as hard as any of them. When the vote to unionize was taken, Perdue won by a landslide. He had successfully defended his corporate turf by proving, despite his salary, that he was one of the guys.

But the story doesn't stop there. He later testified to the President's Commission on Organized Crime that in the heat of battle he had tried to get mob boss Paul Castellano to fight the union with him. Frank said those conversations with the godfather of one of New York's notorious Five Families never went anywhere, and that he deeply regretted having had them. There is no evidence to the contrary, so we'll take him at his word, and we certainly aren't condoning such behavior. Our point is that if "it takes a tough man to raise a tender chicken" hadn't been true at more than one level, it wouldn't have played so well for all those years.

Perdue had the three qualities a corporate hero needs.

- In his ads he came across as someone like us, someone his customers had already grown to trust—their local butcher.
- He listened to what we had to tell him about what we wanted and was fiercely, even obsessively, committed to doing what it took to give it to us.
- As a person, he was complex enough to hold our interest for the twenty years his ads would have to run on prime time for him to successfully build his brand. That consistency of message is another important part of being a corporate hero. The hero provides the stability that lets the business grow. And in Frank's case, his chickens really were good.

*   *   *

Harlan Sanders is another southern gentleman who built his fortune by proudly loving chickens (that sounds more salacious than we intended, but you catch the drift). In the 1930s, Harlan began selling deep-fried chicken out behind his filling station in Corbin, Kentucky, a small town about a two-hour drive from Louisville. He was constantly adjusting his spices and tinkering with his recipe to give his customers just what they wanted—things were slow on that back road, so he had plenty of time to talk to them about it—until he came up with his famous "11 secret herbs and spices." Word spread. The governor of the state dropped by and liked what he ate enough to make Harlan a member of the Honorable Order of Kentucky Colonels in 1935, which is why we know Harlan as Colonel Sanders, and his process as Kentucky Fried Chicken.

Harlan got some national fame—in 1939, his chicken shack was mentioned in food critic Duncan Hines's guidebook *Adventures in Good Eating*—but like many of the most creative cultural entrepreneurs he seemed content to remain the best at what he did for a small but appreciative audience. If you work for a cutting-edge creative shop, you know the attractions of that position. And there Harlan's story would have ended if fate, in the form of Interstate 75, hadn't stepped in. When Harlan realized the new highway would take away the drive-by business he depended on, he took to the road himself. Financed only with his $105 monthly Social Security checks, he drove through the South giving away samples of his chicken and signing up franchisees. Since he was meeting a lot of strangers, he had to dress up, and this is when he adopted his trademark white suit and black string tie, and had his white goatee neatly trimmed. An image that became iconic. In 1964, he sold his business, which now had over six hundred franchisees, to a conglomerate (it is currently part of Yum! Brands) and retired. Because his name and face were so associated with the product, and because no one could sell fried chicken half as well as he could, the new owners kept him on as corporate spokesman.

It's a nice Horatio Alger poor-boy-makes-good tale. The sort of bedtime story you tell MBAs, but Colonel Sanders was not yet a full-on corporate hero. To reach that exalted status, he had to catch us by surprise. When the new owners changed his recipe for gravy, he hated their concoction and came out swinging. He very publicly called the gravy "sludge" and said the mashed potatoes tasted "like wallpaper paste." That is not how your typical corporate spokesman describes the product. It got our attention. So did the parent company, when it sued him for breach of contract—he was after all still being paid a very handsome salary to say nice things about them. Then he countersued them for defamation of character! It was his face on the bucket saying that what was inside was "finger lickin' good." If it weren't, they were making him personally look bad! It deeply offended his sense of southern honor, to say nothing about his highly developed sense of taste.

A legal furball ensued that generated lots of free publicity, but more important for future sales, the struggle established that Colonel Sanders cared deeply about the quality of his product. So deeply that he was willing to risk everything to make sure we got what he promised. It was all about trust. That loyalty was appreciated and returned. In 1974, Colonel Sanders was ranked the number two best-known celebrity worldwide. Today, his is the only portrait that hangs across from that of Chairman Mao on Beijing's Tiananmen Square. That is brand recognition money can't buy.

So what do our three heroes—Buffett, Perdue, and Sanders—have in common other than having become very, very wealthy by doing what they love doing? Not a bad thing for us to emulate after all. For one thing, each personifies, in an almost mystical way, a core quality of their business.

Buffett's style of value investing requires him to look past the glitz and accounting razzle-dazzle of corporate reports to see the real intrinsic worth of the companies he invests in. His personal commitment to staying "just plain folks" isn't an affectation—it allows him to remain grounded and balanced so that he can recognize other companies that share his view on long-term growth. His ability to let his shareholders know that he considers them to be his partners and sees their economic concerns as equal to his own is central to the stability that has allowed Berkshire Hathaway to trounce the S&P 500 for forty-one of the last forty-five years.

One of Frank Perdue's innovations in poultry production was his keeping the lights on in the chicken house and feeding his birds twenty-two hours a day to promote faster growth. They weren't the only ones staying up late. He himself was a notorious workaholic who had a bed installed in his office to make it easier to be near his desk around the clock, even though his home was only fifty yards away.

And Colonel Harlan Sanders really did love serving people chicken. He totally got off on it. He used to travel with insulated luggage filled with fried chicken so that he could offer the other passengers on his plane some of his original recipe. We know this because one of us, when he was in middle school, was once on a plane with Colonel Sanders. After standing up and announcing who he was, the Colonel had the stewardess serve his chicken. Then he went from seat to seat asking everyone how they liked it. And he really listened to the answer. When he got to us, we said his chicken was good but that our mother cooked fried chicken every Sunday at our house and we liked hers better. He smiled and responded, "Good. That's how it's supposed to be. You say hello to your mom for me." Now *that* is truly gracious southern hospitality. Just the sort of attitude you want to have when your friends come over unexpectedly around dinnertime. Luckily, you can buy it by the bucket.

The quality that connects your hero to your product isn't something you can add on later. It is inherent in the character of the hero you choose. And it has to be authentic, because we'll be trying your hero's point of view on for size, and if there is anything phony about it we will know it right away. It will make our skin crawl. It is hard to define in advance who is the right hero for your story, but you will know your hero when you see him or her, because a good hero is magnetic. A great hero is almost impossible to take your eyes off of. Just look around. Your company, or your client's, is filled with heroes that will fill the bill.

* * *

One problem we often have with our clients is that they are reluctant to take the role of hero. They say to us, "My customers are my heroes; shouldn't they be the hero of my stories too?" It is a good point. The hero needs to be equal to your customers, but that equality works both ways. Your customer is your hero, and you need to be your customer's as well. If your story doesn't include that, there is a very real danger that you, the storyteller, will end up in a passive, reactive position. The deal won't close. The idea won't sell. The meeting will end with everyone having a warm and rosy glow, but no real business will have been done. Remember, your customer doesn't know where your story is going—you do. You are both in the same car, but someone has to drive. Don't be afraid to take the wheel. Heroes are always active.

So, when you are putting together your story to persuade your clients that your company, your product, or your idea is the right one, choose a hero that is just like them, only maybe a little better. Let your hero take a stand for what is right and hold it, so they know they can trust him; then let the hero surprise them. If your story has that kind of hero, we'll follow him all the way to your bank.

One thing all three of our heroes have in common is that they are all good listeners, and listening is a big part of their storied success. If your story is going to contain a hero equal to your customers, you have to know who your customers are. As Dale Carnegie once said, "To sell Jane Doe what Jane Doe wants to buy, you must see the world through Jane Doe's eyes."

* * *

Active listening, a technique pioneered by psychologists Carl Rogers and Richard Farson, has gained wider and wider acceptance in business and education since it was first developed in the sixties. In essence, it is listening to *understand* the other person's point of view, not to either agree or disagree with it. As Farson said in their seminal paper, "Active Listening," "Despite the popular notion that listening is a passive approach, clinical and research evidence clearly show that sensitive listening is a most effective agent for individual change and group development. . . . People who have been listened to in this way become more emotionally mature, more open to their experiences, less defensive, more democratic, and less authoritarian." Put simply, actively listening to your clients makes them better people. And it is a two-way street; knowing how to actively listen will make you better, too.

It is not hard to do, but it takes practice. To master the technique takes years, but even the first steps will show positive results. Here is what we recommend.

First, work on listening for your client's whole story, not just the facts that it contains. Stories are facts wrapped in emotions, after all. The facts we get quickly, but at the same time your client is sending a lot of emotional information as well—through body language, facial expressions, and the rhythm, pitch, and tone of his or her voice. To get all that information, we suggest you practice running down a mental checklist.

Next time you are in a meeting where you don't have to be

doing that much talking, watch your client for specific things he is doing to communicate nonverbally.

1. What is his overall body language saying? Is he leaning forward or back? Are his shoulders slumped, tight, what? Are his feet flat on the floor, or does he have his legs crossed? If crossed, are his thighs together or is his pelvis opened out and relaxed? Are his elbows close to the body? Are his arms folded across his chest? All of these body postures are saying something. Don't think about it, just take it in. One way to do this is to put your own body in his position and see how it feels. But be careful. This is somewhat like a neurolinguistic programming technique known as modeling in which you try to influence and manipulate a conversation by copying your listener's body language. *What we are suggesting is absolutely not that!* The whole point of active listening is that you aren't manipulating or trying to control anything. You are just listening to understand. Understanding your client's body language is part of that.

2. Observe how your client is using his hands to emphasize points or to hide moments of nervousness or indecision. Pay particular attention to moments when he looks at his own hands. Such moments often indicate that he is grappling with the issue internally or is about to reach a decision. But again, the point isn't to control the situation. It is simply to observe.

3. Let the sound of the person's voice play over you like music. Not the words, just the tone, resonance, timbre, and cadence. What voices from your own past does his voice remind you of? Let your mind wander a bit; let the sound of your client's voice connect you to emotions you have felt before. His tone of voice is clearly telling you how he feels about what he is saying. Voice stress analysis is the technique used in the best lie detectors. It is a skill we have all been developing since childhood. If you pay attention to your own feelings, you are much better at it than any machine. Does your client feel happy, sad, concerned, aggressive, amused? You don't have to respond. All you have to do is what you do with good music—listen and appreciate.

4. Be aware of the expression on the speaker's face. Human expressions are universal. People show their feelings the same way in Borneo as they do in Brooklyn. A study done by Paul Ekman at the University of California, San Francisco, showed photos of New Guinea natives experiencing basic emotional states to his graduate students. The students correctly identified the emotion the natives were feeling, despite the face paint and other distracting elements. The experiment was reversed. The New Guinea tribesmen had no problem saying what emotions young children in Berkeley were feeling. So facial expression transcends culture. In the business world, many of us have been trained to keep a "poker face" so

as not to give away our negotiating positions and real bottom lines, and that tends to become a habit. Not to worry. No one can totally control the small muscles that surround the eyes, nostrils, mouth, and chin. Microtensions here reveal the expressions that are struggling to come out. But you have to be very quiet internally to "hear" what your client's face is trying to say to you if he is working to keep it hidden. If you are busy thinking up a clever reply to his last comment, you will miss the lion's share of what he has to say. That is why we recommend you begin practicing this sort of listening when you don't have to be constantly responding. Eventually, this will become second nature. You can walk and chew gum at the same time.

5. Finally, look your client square in the eyes. There is an old saying, "The eyes are the window of the soul." What is the quality of your client's gaze? Is it excited, bored, piercing, twinkling with amusement, or just taking it all in? You need to know. But be careful. Looking directly into someone's eyes can be taken as aggressive. In some cultures, it is past rude; it is dangerous. That is why so many people have their faces buried in newspapers as they ride the subways. But in business, it is worth taking the risk. But first, be sure to soften your own gaze. Make sure your eyes are open and nonjudgmental. Remind yourself that you are actively listening to understand, not to control or score points. It always helps us to

remember Humphrey Bogart's eyes in the last scene of *Casablanca*. He has just shot down the Nazi villain in cold blood and looks over toward his friend Louis, a French cop who now has Bogart's fate in his hands. It is a great look. Then Louis says, "Round up the usual suspects," and Bogie's eyes just take it in and profoundly relax in that wonderful world-weary, knowing way he had. But you have your own movie heroes. Choose one and remember how his eyes look in their best moments when they weren't pushing, they were just seeing. Having a fifty-foot eyeball to study and emulate is one more reason to actually go out to the movies. The other is the popcorn.

If you've been keeping count, yes, there are five things (other than content) we suggest you be aware of when you are listening to your client, just as there are five story elements, and that is not a coincidence. We could go into this in much greater detail (with our clients, we sometimes do), but let's keep it simple for now. With just a little practice, this checklist can become second nature, but running through it in the heat of a high-stakes business meeting, where you need to respond to your client's concerns while still keeping the meeting on track so that it ends the way you want it to, is a lot to handle. It can feel like you are juggling chain saws as you walk a tightrope. And we still haven't gotten to the part where you check to see if you actually have heard what is being said correctly. That is the real key to active listening.

So we suggest you practice this next exercise in low-stakes situations first. Eventually, it will slip into your business repertoire effortlessly.

Working with a friend, partner, or peer (maybe someone on your creative team; this tends to build team cohesion), discuss a subject you both feel strongly about. Take turns stating your positions. When your partner has had her say, repeat back to her what you heard. Don't parrot it; put it in your own words. Then ask if you got it right. You probably got some of it. Work on your version of her view until she agrees you got it all. Then it's your turn to tell your story. Help her hear it. Make sure she is hearing what you say accurately and is hearing all that you say. Do this a few times back and forth and you'll notice that you not only become more sensitive to each other's point of view, but you're also moving toward agreement. Active listening promotes understanding. Understanding leads to a sense of equality. Equality promotes trust. And in the business world, trust is money in the bank.

Trust us. This exercise really works. Don't stop doing it. The more you do it, the more it works. Make it part of your team's regular routine. It is a great way to tune up before important pitch meetings.

CHAPTER FIVE

Finding Common Ground

If our five-element model defines the hero as the point of view of the story, the person who allows us to enter into the story and see it through his or her eyes, what happens to the hero's traditional role? You know, slaying dragons, rescuing damsels in distress, and vanquishing bad guys? All the things we expect our action heroes to do in a Saturday matinee. Well, the hero still does all that. In fact, in real life, heroes do it precisely by providing the point of view that brings people together, makes them feel equal and equally part of finding a solution to their problem, and then leading the charge to get it done. Just ask the United States Marines. They have been doing that for over two hundred years, and in doing it they have created one of the most effective brands in history, a brand identification so strong that they can quite accurately say there is no such thing as an ex-marine.

In describing the Marine Corps as a brand, we are aware we are on somewhat shaky ground. The intense feelings of loyalty, dedication, and sacrifice with which marines surround the fact of their service far exceeds those extended to any commercial product, which from our standpoint makes their story more powerful and interesting. After all, no one has died defending the honor of Starbucks or Nike. But the Marine Corps *is* a brand in the sense that it is competing with the other three armed services for the same demographic group—young men and women seeking to serve their country in time of need. All four services have defined marketing strategies to reach out to those "customers" and bring them in. That the Marines seem to do this best is all the more reason to understand just how they do it. The fact that the Marines transcend brand doesn't mean the Corps can't help us define what a brand is and understand how to create one.

Walk into any Marine officer's office on any base around the world and you will be surrounded by pieces of history adorning the walls—signed unit flags from Vietnam, equipment that saw action in Korea, trophies won on the long island-hopping march across the Pacific during World War II—as well as the personal artifacts that the officer has collected on his or her tours around the world. This is a conscious communication strategy. When a marine comes in and snaps to attention in front of the officer's desk, he is surrounded by tangible evidence of what links the officer and himself and, regardless of rank, makes them equal. They are both marines, both part of a warrior tradition that they are committed above all else to upholding. That is the story the walls tell.

That shared story is with each marine from the moment he gets dressed in the morning. Every element of the Marine Corps uniform (the visible signage of their brand) is connected to an heroic event of the past. The red stripe that runs down the legs of the corporal's dress trousers honors the blood spilled in the Battle of Chapultepec—the famous "halls of Montezuma" in "The Marine Hymn." The ivory-handled Mamluk sword you see on recruiting ads is a symbol of the fierce hand-to-hand fighting against the Barbary pirates on the shores of Tripoli. Ask any marine about Iwo Jima, Chosin Reservoir, or Khe Sanh and his tone of voice will change as he answers. Those victories are historical facts, but the subtle emotions with which they are told—a sense of shared sacrifice, common courage, and pride in belonging—are what make the Marine Corps legendary.

Our point is that as important as it is to have a corporate hero like Warren Buffett or Colonel Sanders who can tell your story in a way that opens it up and lets your clients in, it is even more important to have a story that your own team can actively live and embody. Stories that are just words will only last as long as the next news cycle. Stories that are made physical, that you and your team actually try on for size every day and then embody—those are the stories that become lifestyles and create brands. In fact, finding such a story is the one thing you can do that actually helps you create a brand. All the rest is mostly just advertising razzle-dazzle and wishful thinking (and besides, everyone else is trying the same tricks you are).

Harley-Davidson, Nike, Apple, and Starbucks became successful brands because their direct-contact sales force lives the stories that make them great. When that happens, a story becomes almost telepathically quick to spread because—in ways that are hardwired into our nervous system that we'll talk more about later in this chapter—embodied stories are incredibly attractive. People want to belong to that kind of brand.

That is one reason why despite the fact that being a Marine Corps lance corporal—the leader of a multiman fire team that is the first inside when they kick down the front door and clear a house of insurgents during urban combat— is far and away the most dangerous job in Iraq, the Corps continues to meet its recruitment goals without having to lower its standards. There is a direct connection between finding and sharing the right story and building and growing a brand that can occupy territory—whether that territory is shelf space, something more ephemeral but equally profitable in cyberspace, or the actual boots-on-the-ground physical space that the Marine Corps specializes in taking and holding against all comers. As Colonel Bob Hayes, the deputy chief of operations and training at Parris Island says, "We have two missions in the Marine Corps—to win battles and make marines." We actually think that's just one job. As history shows, if you make the marines, winning battles is a natural result. So how do they do it?

Every Thursday, a little before 10:00 AM, a crowd of civilians begins to form at the south end of the parade deck at the

United States Marine Corps Recruit Depot in San Diego. It is an eclectic group drawn from cities large and small across the United States. Depending on the day, you'll see everything from suit-and-tie formal wear to full biker colors—we even saw one elderly gentleman in an elegant purple silk zoot suit the day we went. These are the family and friends of young marine recruits who are about to complete their boot camp and undergo the "Eagle, Globe and Anchor" ceremony that transforms them from "some sort of grab-ass amphibious life form [a drill instructor's description, not ours] into an actual Marine." Like all true initiations, it is simple, deeply moving, and permanent. As their commanding officer tells them, "Once you become a marine, no one can ever take that away from you." It is an intensely personal moment, shared between the new marine and the drill instructor that helped to mold him, but like all good marketers the Corps understands that the power of its brand comes from the ripple effect of the story the brand contains, so these families have been invited to attend. As the one Marine sergeant told us, "We recruit the marine, but we enlist the whole family."

You hear them before you see them—the sound of quick cadence calls and the perfectly timed slap of boots on concrete. Six platoons of recruits in shorts and green T-shirts come around a corner at the far end of the large open space running in tight formation behind their platoon colors. They arrive, then in perfect unison snap to attention. There is a moment of slightly awed silence. This is the first time these parents have seen their sons in three months. Having just completed the most demanding basic training in the military, these recruits, averaging only eighteen years of age, are in the best physical shape of their lives. They stand straight and tall, broad shoulders back, chins in, eyes level, and somehow make that position seem completely natural and relaxed. One drill instructor told us, "We've had parents who didn't recognize their sons at first. We have had more than a few claim we have stretched their kid somehow." These young men look great. More than that, they look ready. They clearly are alert, relaxed, and mentally quick. If you spend any time around a Marine base you will constantly hear the phrase "good to go." You look at these recruits and you know what that means.

To those of us who haven't been through it, boot camp is often thought of as a process of stripping away the recruits' individual identities so that a new Marine Corps identity can be mechanically stamped on. In fact, it is a great deal more than that. The recruits know who they really are much more completely at the end of boot camp than they did at the beginning. Partially, this is because they know more about the man on their left and the man on their right and so have come to know a great deal about themselves as well, and, partially, it is because they have been tested, and tested themselves, in ways they didn't think possible three months before, but we think it is largely because they have found in the traditions and legends of the Corps a story that has allowed them to experience and refine their own moral core. That is one of the things warrior stories have been doing since Homer first sang of the exploits of fleet-footed Achilles on the shores of Troy. It is part of the power of story, and part of why these recruits are standing so straight and tall. It is a large reason why the

Marine Corps is known not only as "the first to fight" (a semi-official motto that they take very seriously), but also as the first to innovate (which is another reason for us to be studying their brand model).

No one wants to be depending on a human robot in combat. You want a flesh-and-blood, fast-thinking hero next to you when the shooting starts. To make sure that is what you get, every marine completes "the Crucible" as the defining experience of their training.

The Crucible is a grueling fifty-four-hour test of individual stamina and unit performance, something like a final exam. The entire platoon either passes or fails as a unit. During these two and a half days, the recruits will march over forty miles on less than four hours of sleep while carrying a seventy-pound pack, eat only two and a half cold prepackaged meals, and negotiate thirty combat-simulating tasks, such as evacuating a wounded comrade or engaging in a night firefight. Twelve of these tasks involve what are called "warrior stations."

When the recruits arrive at a warrior station, they find a large picture of a decorated marine—often a Medal of Honor winner—and the award citation that tells that marine's story. For example—station five is called "Day's Defense," after Corporal James L. Day, who earned the Medal of Honor for action on Okinawa. For three days, despite being wounded himself, Corporal Day held a key ridge against repeated enemy assaults, aided only by those few wounded marines he managed to pull to safety. As a result, a key battle was won and many more marines' lives were saved. After reading this citation to the recruits, who are already exhausted by their previous tasks, the drill instructor tells them to set up a defensive position and maintain it against simulated attack.

The platoon is trying on Corporal Day's heroism for size. It is the DI's job to make sure it fits. He is constantly asking, "Are you tired? You thirsty? Don't you think Day was? Did it stop him? You going to let it stop you? No way, marines don't stop! We don't give up!" It works. The recruits keep going, keep fighting, long past anything they thought they would have been able to do. The story of Corporal Day's heroism, and their own story of completing the Crucible, becomes inextricably linked. The legends of the past forge the heroes of the future.

Of all the stations we saw, it was station twelve that was most powerful and transforming. It is appropriately named "Core Values." It is just a simple hut in the middle of the desert. The recruits file in and are told to be seated. Then, for the first time in their training, their DI sits down with them. Up until now, they have only seen him standing, and usually leaning toward them a little too close for comfort. Even more shocking, he takes off the distinctive broad-brimmed campaign hat that lets the whole world know what he is and what he does. It is a testament to how controlled the boot camp experience is that the recruits immediately react to the new level of intimacy and vulnerability. They don't like it. You can see on their faces that they are thinking, "Oh, jeez, how did we screw up now? This has got to be bad!"

When the DI speaks, it isn't his familiar staccato bark. Now his voice is actually warm and resonant though it still has a bit of cadence march singsong in it. He explains that the schedule gives them twenty minutes to get to know each other. He is going to ask them a series of questions. They are going to answer. Do they understand? In unison they shout back, "Aye, sir!" Then he methodically asks each recruit their name and where they are from. Each in turn crisply answers: "James Estes, Freemont, Texas." "Louis Mendez, East Los Angeles." "Henry Cobb, Portland, Oregon." "Tim Pitkin, Plainfield, Vermont."

When they have finished, the DI says, "So, we are all from the same place, right?"

There is a moment of confusion. The DI repeats, "We are all from the same place, right? We are all Americans, right?"

In unison, they shout back they are. With that, things relax. You even see a few smiles. For the next few minutes, and for the first time in their training, they are just men taking a very focused break getting to know each other. At the end of the twenty minutes allowed, the DI makes the point: "It is the man on your left, the man on your right that is going to get you through this. Get to know him. It matters. It can make all the difference. Here, in combat, for the rest of your life."

The core value of the Corps is that level of trust, equality, and simple honesty. It is a deeply moral core value because, as one Marine sergeant told us, "Morality is waking up in the morning and doing your job so someone else won't have to do it for you," which is as good a description as we have come across. It is the ability of these men to feel equal to each other that makes them able to sacrifice for a common goal, and that makes them true heroes.

* * *

Human beings didn't get to the top of the food chain by being the jungle's roughest and toughest. and your company or team won't get the big contracts by advertising muscle alone. What will make the difference is your ability to bond and work together. It is more than just strength in numbers. The biggest army doesn't always win. Otherwise, we would all be speaking Russian. It is the army that fights as one and can coordinate its attack that usually gains victory. The same is true in business. The biggest and best story in the world won't cut it if your whole team isn't on board and telling it as their own—and know it so well that they are constantly changing it in ways that keep it fresh and relevant.

To create this unit dynamic, the Marines spend days doing close-order drill. They march back and forth across the parade deck to quick commands and execute elaborate patterns until they literally dream about them at night (as we'll see later, those dreams are a big part of locking those patterns into memory). As civilians, this always seemed an enormous waste of time to us. It is so—well, uncreative. But as we started looking into it, we realized that we were completely and totally wrong.

Since the time when three hundred Spartans held off an army of over 1.5 million Persians for three days by standing shoulder to shoulder at Thermopylae, it has been known that this sort of training is crucial to success in combat. And as we'll see, close-proximity physical tuning is also a big reason for the bonding that lies at the core of brands with core constituencies as different as Starbucks and Harley-Davidson. Because bonding is such a primary survival characteristic for our species, it makes sense that we would have special neural circuitry dedicated to maintaining it, but until a young lab assistant at the University of Parma walked into the lab of Dr. Giacomo Rizzolatti eating an ice cream cone, no one knew how powerful these circuits actually were.

At the time, Rizzolatti and his associates Leonardo Fogassi and Vittorio Gallese were studying the specific neurons that macaque monkeys use when they grasp their food. This involved inserting electrodes directly into the brain of a monkey, then getting the monkey to grasp a peanut. If they had the electrode in exactly the right place, a buzzer would sound. Then they would move the electrode very slightly and repeat. If the buzzer sounded again, they were following the neural circuit. It was a slow, painstaking process, but gradually it was yielding a detailed map of the neural network involved, the sort of methodical grunt work that most basic science involves. But when a lab assistant returned from a break holding an ice cream cone, things suddenly got world-class interesting. The buzzer linked up to the monkey started to sound.

The monkey wasn't holding on to anything. The buzzer shouldn't have sounded, obviously a mistake. So the lab tech put down his ice cream cone to check the equipment. The buzzer stopped. Satisfied it was just an equipment glitch, he picked up the ice cream cone again. The buzzer sounded again, even louder.

Observing the monkey closely, Rizzolatti realized that the monkey was reacting to his assistant's grasping of the ice cream cone as if the monkey itself were grasping it! And not in a general way. The monkey wasn't having an emotional response to the ice cream (or at least that wasn't what was being measured) but was reacting to the opening and closing of the assistant's hand on a deeply physical level. The same pattern of neurons were firing in the monkey's brain when it saw another primate performing the action of grasping as fired when it was itself doing the action directly.

It isn't supposed to work like that. At the level of neural structure that Rizzolatti was studying, the brain's parts have very specific tasks. One group of neurons reacts only to horizontal lines. Another separate group reacts only to vertical. The neurons they were mapping open and close the monkey's hands, and that is all they are supposed to do. But now the monkey's hand was not physically grasping anything, and yet these neurons were still firing. The monkey was clearly imitating the lab tech's actions, but was doing it at a purely mental level.

For the first time, cognitive scientists were watching the transfer of pure knowledge—the learning of a task by nothing more than observation—at a hardware, not a software, level. They had stumbled onto the wiring that allows us all to learn by imitation. We knew that it existed. Babies only twelve hours old will react to your sticking out your tongue by sticking out their own tongue. We know that children learn by copying the actions of their parents and friends, and that imitation is not only the sincerest form of flattery but also the most effective teaching strategy. We know it so well we don't even think of it as amazing, but it is. And once you know where in the brain that ability is located and start to study it closely, it becomes even more amazing.

It was a stunning achievement. Rizzolatti named these neurons "mirror neurons" because they allow us to mentally mirror, and so understand, the actions of others. "It took us several years to believe what we were seeing," he recently said, but the time spent proving his hypothesis—that mirror neurons were involved in building and maintaining an internal mental map that allows us not only to learn from but to anticipate the actions of others—was very well spent. As he points out, "We are exquisitely social creatures. Our survival depends on understanding the actions, intentions, and emotions of others. Mirror neurons allow us to grasp the mind of others not through conceptual reasoning, but through direct simulation. By feeling, not by thinking."

Mirror neurons are why when you are watching a ball game and see the batter swing hard and knock it out of the park, you get a little rush of dopamine as if you had hit the homer yourself. As far as some parts of your brain are concerned, you did. Mirror neurons are why you will see everyone in a sports bar cringe when the tight end takes a brutally hard hit as he is pulling in a pass (and you thought it was just because everyone had money on the game—well, OK, that, too). You don't even need to know the rules of football to react that way. Recent studies have demonstrated that mirror neurons connected to the shoulder and arm fire in people who see a professional tennis player make a powerful serve even if they have never played tennis. But if the viewer is a tennis player, his or her reaction is more profound and focused. So mirror neurons, like other sorts of mirrors, can be polished.

Mirror neurons are not solely associated with sight. A specific set of audio mirror neurons will fire in response to sounds—which is why the sound of a bottle of beer opening during a radio commercial is so strangely satisfying. Another set of specially dedicated mirror neurons allow us to understand the emotions of others not simply by picking up on and decoding a long list of visual and auditory cues (which would take far too long to be really useful), but by directly experiencing their emotional states as if they were our own.

When Bill Clinton said, "I feel your pain," he wasn't kidding. He could do it because he had spent years as a professional politician polishing precisely those mirror neurons and keeping them in top working order. If these neurons are not functioning properly for whatever reason, we have an impaired sense of empathy—and an enormous amount of research is now being done to explore whether malfunctioning mirror neurons are one of the causes of autism, and if so, what can be done to help.

That link of mirror neurons with empathy (and the connection of mirror neurons with grasping and taking—particularly grasping that is associated with eating) has a lot to do with branding. It is one reason why researchers now have volunteers getting brain scans as they watch the new commercials shown on Super Bowl Sunday. By studying the response of mirror neurons, the corporate researchers hope to find out which commercials really work.

But what is most amazing about mirror neurons is that

they allow us to read each other's minds. Well, in a manner of speaking. Research done by Marco Iacoboni at UCLA has shown that our mirror neurons react differently when we see a person pick up a cup to take a sip of tea than when the same person picks up the cup to clean off the table. And this difference is present before we consciously know which action the person is about to take. Two almost identical films were shown to a group of students. In both, a hand came into view and reached for a cup on a table. The film was stopped and the student was asked, "Will the person take a sip of tea, or put the cup on a tray to be cleaned away?" Visually, the hands were in almost identical positions. But in numbers far greater than accountable for by chance, the students knew which action was about to be taken. They didn't *see* what was coming; they knew what was coming because in the mental model of the world they had constructed with their mirror neurons, they felt themselves about to do it. Mirror neurons are intimately involved—possibly primarily responsible for— our ability to know the intentions of others.

Which brings us back to the Marine Corps. When a Marine lance corporal on the mean streets of Fallujah rounds a corner and sees a young boy lifting his hand, he needs to *know*—not guess and certainly not think about—what that boy intends to do. Lives depend on it. The marine is conditioned to make the right choice (the boy was actually raising his hand in a friendly greeting, so a life was spared) because of all the time he spent polishing the associated mirror neurons at boot camp, and later running simulations of street sweeps and house-to-house searches.

All the close-order drill early in their career is one reason that a platoon's mirror neurons are so exquisitely tuned to one another. Walking that quickly, that close together, if you don't let your mirror neurons engage and take over, you are going to have a collision—and then your DI is going to ream you royally. It doesn't take too many times before you get with the program. Pretty soon you are allowing parts of your mind that work faster than your conscious thoughts to come to the fore as you physically anticipate the actions of the man on your left and the man on your right. The more you do that, the easier it is for you to anticipate their emotional reactions as well, and the stronger the bond of empathy that links you to all the other heroes of the Corps—past, present, and even future.

And it is enjoyable. Evolution has seen the survival advantages of this sort of physical coordination (it is how humans hunt as well as how we protect our territory), and so it gives you a little jolt of pleasure when you do it right. That is why people like to square-dance and why most cultures have mating rituals that involve coordinated group movement. We have audio and emotional mirror neurons as well, but the majority of our mirror neurons are dedicated to sensing and modeling physical movements. So the best way to stimulate empathy is by doing physical actions together.

What fascinates us as corporate communicators is how often rapid movement while in close physical contact is associated with the development of a successful brand. We believe this is because of mirror neuron tuning.

Take Starbucks. We love to go in there because everyone behind the counter always seems happy. And that is despite the fact they are constantly engaged in a hectic and elaborate high-speed dance in which they bob and weave around each other while performing a series of complicated actions, all the time holding thin paper containers of scalding liquid. Delicious and highly aromatic scalding liquid, true, but collide and spill it on yourself and it is the scalding part you'll remember. But the crew at Starbucks never seems to collide. And they don't seem to be actively keeping an eye on each other either. They have done it together so long that it is "second nature," and they happily let the neurons that are dedicated to handling this sort of thing (their mirror neurons) anticipate each other's intentions while their higher brain functions soak in the satisfied smiles of customers getting their first strong caffeine hit of the day. What Starbucks has set up is a self-sustaining positive feedback loop based on close physical proximity and mirror neurons.

The same sort of physical feedback loop is one of the drivers of Harley-Davidson's phenomenal success. Every weekend you will find Harley owners getting together in front of their local sales outlet and then roaring off for a run out into the country. These trips are good for everyone. It makes marketing sense for the retailers because while the riders are waiting for enough other owners to show up to make the trip worthwhile, they spend time shopping for what they need to make the trip more comfortable—often clothing that proudly displays the Harley logo. For the riders, there is a definite survival advantage—the number one cause of accidents to motorcycle riders is drivers who don't see them and suddenly change lanes. It is very hard for a driver not to see a pack of ten or more Harleys. Put together fifty or more—as we often see in our neck of the woods—and it is hard not to pull over and just enjoy the parade.

And there are a lot of mirror neurons involved. As the riders are driving in a pack, they constantly need to make adjustments to stay in their place in the formation. They are tuning themselves to anticipate each other's actions the same way that the crew at Starbucks does, and with the same result. It is enjoyable. And as they do, they soak in the positive reactions of the people they pass. We have been told by riders we trust that everyone—cops included—smiles at you when you are in a group of Harleys riding by. Put together a large enough group of Harley riders—as Jay Leno does every year to support local charities here in Los Angeles—and it can feel as if the whole town is on happy juice.

At this point, we need to stress that there are two separate phenomena that go by the name "brand." One of these—which we'll call a logo brand—has to do with providing security and consistency. These are brands like Coca-Cola. You buy Coke because you like the taste and know that wherever you are in the world, it is going to taste the same. You stay at a Hilton because you know what you will be getting and don't want any surprises spoiling your business trip. You look for the

logo because is the seal of approval and sign of consistent performance. For this type of brand, the five-element story model
is most helpful in letting you see the characteristics your hero
spokesperson will need in order to give your logo the right
sort of moral authority.

The other type of brand we'll call lifestyle brands. These
are brands that people embrace because they want to be with
people who share the same lifestyle as themselves. These
brands are all about bonding and nets of empathy. When I
drive a Harley, I am doing a lot more than choosing a type
of transportation; I'm also choosing the friends I'm going to
be riding with and the sorts of stories I'm going to be sharing
with them later. Lifestyle brands are more stable than logo
brands precisely because my investment in my lifestyle is so
extensive. I am much less likely to change all my friends than
to change my preference in the taste of toothpaste. For this
sort of brand, one of the most important things our story
model has to offer is the understanding that stories well told
stimulate our mirror neurons, and that the best use of story is
not simply to tell it, but to actually get your audience to live
it with you.

If you are Starbucks, your story is "This is how you make a
really good cup of coffee." If I put that story out front and let
the clients see it happening, their mirror neurons will let them
directly experience it. It becomes part of our common lifestyle
because it becomes part of our common life experience. If you
hide the making of the coffee behind a wall, it won't have the
same effect. And the more your story involves physical actions
done close together, the more easily your story will transmit.

It will transmit in an almost telepathic fashion because our mirror neurons are allowing us to anticipate and understand each other's intentions. If those intentions are good, we know it and respond, setting up a positive emotional loop across another dedicated set of mirror neurons.

What can you do to increase this? Get more people involved. This sort of feedback loop gains power exponentially as it grows. How can you do that? Get your core team tuned up and high functioning. If you enjoy doing what you are doing, so will the people you attract into your orbit. Just like the marines doing close-order drill, it is the time spent working closely together that will let you relax, work out the kinks, and get to the fun part. Of course, asking your creative team to come in and put in extra hours working closely on weekends just because it feels good is a nonstarter. But they might very well get together as part of a common charity event—say, a walk or a 10K run that is raising funds for breast cancer, or helping pack up and send off donated clothing to the victims of a natural disaster. Do this sort of thing as a team and it will make your team more attractive across the board.

People like to work for the common good. Like mirror neurons, it seems to be hardwired into us. Look at how many of the lifestyle brands have some charitable connection. Nike supports numerous 10K runs and walks for AIDS and breast cancer, Starbucks is famous for its connection with green causes, and McDonald's (more a logo brand than a lifestyle one, which shows the universality of this point) supports the Ronald McDonald House Charities for kids with cancer and lets us know about it. Making your customers the hero in your story is much more effective when you also allow them an easy way to be heroes in a more traditional way.

Once again, the Marine Corps takes the lead, not only through its Toys for Tots program each Christmas, but in the number of times it is actively involved in staving off disaster. Marine Expeditionary Units (large self-contained fighting teams) are always traveling around the world and always on call. It was an MEU that provided the first aid and shelter to refugees fleeing ethnic cleansing in Kosovo. It was an MEU that got food to the starving children of the Sudan when no one else seemed able to get the warring factions of that troubled country to back off and let the aid arrive. And it was an MEU that got to hardest-hit areas of the Indonesian tsunami in time to save people still trapped in the rubble and then stayed long enough to set up systems to provide safe water and shelter for them once they had been rescued. Though they are "America's First to Fight," the Marines take equal pride in being "the World's 911."

General William Nyland, a former Assistant Commandant of the Corps, explained the deep sense of satisfaction that comes from this. "It is hard to talk about, but one of the incredible gifts that the Marines give those fortunate enough to earn the Eagle, Globe, and Anchor is a chance to be part of something bigger than themselves. Something dedicated to doing good for our nation in peace or in combat. That is really why people join the Marines. That is the blessing the Marines give. All human beings crave that. Few get the opportunity to experience it completely."

One reason we chose the Marines as our core story for this

chapter is that they are exemplars for both types of brands. For more than two hundred years, they have consistently produced warriors at the highest standard. When you send in the U.S. Marines, you know just what you are going to get—victory. And becoming a marine is very much a lifestyle choice. Young men and women become marines not just to serve their country, but also in large measure because they want to be "One of the few, the proud, the Marines."

Jim Lehrer, the PBS anchorman and a marine himself, spoke about the mutually reinforcing dedication that is at the center of a marine's life at the opening ceremony of the National Museum of the Marine Corps near Quantico, Virginia. "It is about the shared experience and the shared knowledge that comes from being a U.S. Marine, such as knowing that you are only as strong and safe as the person on your right and on your left; that a well-trained and motivated human being can accomplish almost anything; that being pushed to do your best is a godsend . . . that 'follow me' really does mean 'follow me' and that 'Semper Fidelis' really does mean 'always faithful.'"

So how does all of this affect our day-to-day jobs of going out and persuading customers or clients that our products or services are the best on the market? Not to be overly crass and commercial, but what's in it for us?

The stories we want you to tell correspond directly with the story behind each and every marine. Heroes stand their ground, and this is certainly true of the marines, who it would be hard not to see as heroic. And corporate heroes—like Colonel Sanders and Frank Perdue—mark out and hold territory in ways that build brands. The heroes of commercial stories always add value to the story, as does Warren Buffett to the story of his corporation. But from a branding standpoint, there is another quality that is even more important. It is the hero who holds your story together and makes it real and exciting for your audience.

Take Indiana Jones. Without him as the hero, *Raiders of the Lost Ark* would be just a collection of confusing action sequences; but because Indiana Jones (what a great Everyman name, right?) is such a compelling hero, everyone wants to see the action through his eyes, and so he holds it all together in a way that makes us take the whole trip without getting lost and confused. What might easily be a hectic hodgepodge of cliffhangers becomes seamlessly understandable. Because it is a physical action movie, the "making it real" is easy even though it is obviously a fantasy. All that running, jumping, and diving out of danger gives our mirror neurons a very pleasant workout. Even though we aren't ourselves doing it, it's almost like we are. Sort of a psychic massage. And because Harrison Ford's performance is so authentic and compelling (and we would say this because the character he is playing isn't perfect; he's terrified of snakes and gets annoyed with himself when he makes a mistake in a way that is both unexpected and obviously right), the story he tells seems real and so becomes part of our reality. We just can't stop thinking about it. Certainly, when we walk out of the theater, we can't stop talking about it. This creates a wave of buzz, but maybe more important, a sense of shared experience with those who saw the film. We enjoy telling them what they themselves just saw, and don't get annoyed when they do the same for us. We are all in it together, all now loyal (some of us rabid) fans. And being part of a group feels good to human beings, so that positively reinforces the story as well. The result is that we are more than ready to go to the sequel, and the Indiana Jones films become a very successful (in this case, a mega-successful) brand. Why? Because the hero was able to make it real for us, and we are continually drawn back to the story when we think about movies we have enjoyed. That is what great heroes do. And it is not coincidence that Indiana Jones ended up selling vast quantities of clothing and apparel so we could all look like him.

Brands extend the reach of your service and product not only in terms of space (by letting it occupy more territory and psychic self space), but also extend it in terms of time (brand loyalty, particularly lifestyle brand loyalty, is by definition more than a momentary fling). Both qualities are central to the commercial success of your stories. The number one trait that is described as leading to the sale of a product or service is reliability. People buy into your story when they know it is real. Your brand story is the stamp of approval that proves that to them. That is what brand has to offer your client.

What's in it for you? You don't want to have to be out there selling the same things to the same people over and over. You want to sell them on your product once and have them stay sold (or better yet, recruit them in telling your story and selling their friends). As the Marines prove, the right story, physically embodied, does that. And that is a big reason why brand value is among the most highly studied asset classes when large corporations merge. Big business knows that the right branding will get you through hard times better than any other asset. Better than cash in the bank, good products on the shelves, or even a clever sales force. Brands are forever.

Senator Mike Mansfield, who was the majority leader in the U.S. Senate longer than any other man, joined the Navy when he was just fourteen and went off to fight in World War I. It was exciting. He was a young boy from Montana serving his country and seeing the world. When his hitch was up, he transferred to the Army and did another year in France before again transferring to the Marine Corps, where he served in combat in the Philippines. Eventually, he retired from the service and, still a very young man, returned to his home in Montana, where he began the long political career that would make him one of Washington's most powerful political figures. He was quite literally the confidant of presidents and kings. But it was his Marine Corps experience that stuck with him.

When he died, at the age of ninety-one, he was buried in Arlington National Cemetery. Anyone can go to visit his grave. It has a simple granite headstone, just one among thousands of others like it. At his request, his epitaph reads simply, "Michael Mansfield, PFC U.S. Marines."

After an incredibly full and eventful life that had taken him to the heights of power and into the center of history, that was all he felt he needed to say for posterity to understand him. He was a marine. That was enough.

So, to sum up. Now that we have seen the power of great brands, how can you get your stories to have that power?

1. First and foremost, see that story is more than just words. As powerful as telling the right story to a client is, it is much, much more powerful if you can get the client to actually live it. Stories are facts wrapped in emotions, and facts physically exist.

2. One way story transmits is across the still-mysterious process of mirror neurons. Get your whole team involved in telling the same story. If you can, tell it broadly and physically. Mirror neurons don't transmit words—they transmit actions and muscular movements best.

3. Don't hide what you do and then deliver it like a magic trick. What you gain from the surprise isn't worth what you are losing. Be open with your process and let your clients in as early as possible so that they get a sense of being part of it all—but, of course, you control the situation. Inviting a client to watch you and your team squabble will be a disaster, but inviting them in once you are working like a well-oiled machine will make them want to join the creative flow. Actually, it will make joining in almost irresistible. And if that flow has a physical

component, all the better. It works for Starbucks—it will work for you.

4. Working together physically is an important part of getting your team to work together across the board. Mirror neurons, remember. Have a sports team, go out and have a picnic, or, better yet, contribute time to a local charity you all agree is worthy (you all have to agree; a top-down edict is poison here) and work together doing something that really matters. The world needs heroes. Go out and give it some. We're not suggesting this from some do-gooder impulse (all right, maybe a little of that, too) but because it makes cold, hard business sense.

5. If you can, get your company story down to a simple phrase or sentence. The Marines did. "Simper Fidelis"—always faithful. Something they each agree to live by. It is a common center that holds them together. Nike did. "Just Do It." Its story is "Lead an active life," and its design teams do just that. They know what runners want because they are runners. But getting it into words isn't as important as getting it into actions you can all do. The Starbucks story is "We make great coffee," and everyone who works there knows how to make a great cup of joe (and to make sure, they practice—each gets a free pound of java every week). If your company does rocket science, make sure everyone knows how to count down from ten and enjoys doing it. Don't let anyone say to you, "That's not my area, I don't do

that." People who say that are usually just insecure about success. One of the functions of a good hero is letting people feel solid and secure, so take the time to help them get it right. Believe us, it will be time well spent. Once your whole team is on the same page, telling—and living—the same story, just like the Marines, you will be unstoppable.

So what should you do now to help build your brand? Well, we are quite serious about getting involved in a common physical activity. One that we have recommended to clients that always seems to work is walks for various good causes, but a company softball team or joining a bowling league are good ideas, too. If you aren't in a position to get everyone to commit, be the first to break the ice; you will be surprised how quickly others join you (which won't hurt your position in the pecking order any). When you do get together, focus on three aspects of the activity.

- Notice how your team working together outside of the normal business hierarchies allows you all to feel more equal (letting people in by feeling equal is a big part of what heroes do), and how this allows good ideas to bubble up from everyone on the team, not simply to trickle down.
- Notice how it gives you a chance to share with one another the stories of your successes. Your company or team has its own heroes. Don't let them fade from memory. Pass their stories on. These types of stories

are particularly important to share with new hires. You can't expect them to tell your team story if they don't know it. Your story is the result of your team's living history—and just like the story of the Marine Corps, it needs to be constantly told to each new recruit so that he sees his own actions in that larger context and so can add to and improve your story.

- Notice how much of a morale booster this sort of activity can be. Working together for the common good will make you all feel better about yourselves and each other. It will show up in your look and feel. And it will give you something positive to talk about with clients should the need arise (it has got to be more interesting than talking about your golf game). If you have a story that grows like that and is told with enthusiasm, it will bring others into your business orbit automatically. Your company or team will become a brand by a process very much like telepathy. People like being with people who like being with each other, particularly if they are good people who like helping other people. It doesn't get simpler than that.

CHAPTER SIX

Sticky Stories:
Memory, Emotions, and Markets

James McGaugh has a dream. In it, he is standing backstage watching his fellow actors perform, waiting for the cue that will send him onstage to play his part, when he suddenly realizes he can't remember any of his lines. Not a single one. The closer the moment for him to step in front of the audience gets, the more elusive his lines become. He feels panic rising from the pit of his stomach. His heart begins to race. His face is flushed, the palms of his hands sweaty. His mouth is dry and swallowing is painful. But no matter how hard he tries he can't remember his lines, he just can't. In fact, the harder he tries to remember, the more his carefully memorized lines seem to retreat. As he hears his cue and feels himself starting to step forward, his panic, and the adrenaline it is releasing into his bloodstream, reach a threshold.

He snaps awake. He is in his bed, in the quiet of the night, feeling his heartbeat begin to decelerate and his breathing return to normal. He has had this dream before.

You have probably had one like it. We know we have, though our particular version adds the wrinkle of also not having on any pants (we know, don't ask). If you have spent any time onstage—and the stage doesn't have to be large; a seat in the corporate boardroom, or a room in which you are standing in front of a screen with a PowerPoint running behind you as you make a presentation to clients, or even an office where you are running through a well-rehearsed pitch to your boss for the raise you so richly deserve is more than large enough—we can almost guarantee you've had some variation of it. As we mentioned in chapter 2, stage fright is a universal. Knowing how to deal with it, and how to use it to your advantage, is a crucial storytelling skill. But there are three things important about James McGaugh's recurring dream we want to bring up now. One, though Dr. McGaugh was initially a theater and music major in college, and so had to memorize hundreds of roles and musical arrangements, he never actually failed to remember his lines. Whatever is going on in this dream, the dream itself is not a memory. Two, this dream is one of the things that led to McGaugh's lifetime interest in how memory really works and to his groundbreaking research into the biochemical and behavioral links between memory and emotion, research he is continuing as founding director of the Center for the Neurobiology of Learning and Memory at the University of California, Irvine, and which has made him one of the world's foremost authorities on the linkage between memory and emotions. Three, as we will see, it may well be that the powerful emotions contained in this dream, and the release of their associated neurotransmitters, are what made him remember his lines so well in the reality.

Obviously, memory is a key to being persuasive. It does you no good to persuade a client of the wisdom of choosing your design if he forgets he had the conversation when he goes into the meeting that will actually give out the contract. And given the number of conversations most decision makers have, that is often the result. It is estimated that each of us receives over thirty-five hundred messages a week—advertisements, phone pitches, stories in the paper, phone calls from our kids. It is no wonder we forget even the important ones. We are all suffering from chronic information overload. And don't think that sending someone a follow-up e-mail will necessarily solve the problem. The typical middle-level corporate executive, the sort of decision maker many of us are trying to persuade, gets an average of 250 e-mails a day. So many e-mails that people are canceling their vacations because the thought of trying to catch up on all of that when they get back after a week in the sun is almost too much to bear. Or worse, they bring along their laptop and spend time on the beach keeping up, managing to do both a slipshod job *and* tick off their significant other (and that's not even mentioning the problem of sand in the keyboard). Of course, as our mothers always told us, a handwritten note makes a good impression, particularly because in the digital age it is so unexpected. Sending one would help maintain the personal contact and sense of equality we spent the last chapter developing, assuming it doesn't get lost in the sea of paper on your contact's desk. A big assumption given that the typical decision maker has over forty hours of backed-up paperwork stacked around her office somewhere.

So the only real solution is to make your story memorable to start with. You need to make it stand out. Your success depends on it. Luckily, the key to doing that is inherent in the nature of story itself. At the risk of sounding like a broken record (a risk we'll gladly take because repetition is one technique for reinforcing memory), STORIES ARE FACTS WRAPPED IN EMOTIONS, and the key to remembering a fact is to anchor it in an emotion. That is why Jerome Bruner estimates that a fact is twenty times more likely to be remembered if it is part of a story (or as he refers to it, anchored in narrative). Given our overload, if it isn't connected to a story (and it isn't something like a phone number we use regularly), it will simply slip our mind. To understand why this is, we need to understand how memories are actually made. That brings us back to Dr. McGaugh.

Our modern, scientific understanding of memory starts with forgetting. In 1949, it was discovered that patients receiving electroshock treatments suffered from selective amnesia. They not only forgot things that happened after receiving a powerful jolt of electricity—when their brains might be expected to be a bit scrambled—they also forgot things that had happened to them before the shock—on their way into the room, or even earlier in the day. This wasn't that surprising. Boxers who are knocked out in the ring routinely fail to remember the punch that took them down, and quite often the round that preceded it. If you have ever suffered from a light concussion, you know it takes a while to remember what was happening before the incident, and you might never remember. This is because memory is not instantaneous. Our memories aren't like photographs—snapped once, then filed away. They are more like computer animation. It takes time for the information to be rendered.

Our senses are constantly taking in a vast amount of data—the words on this page, the color of the page, the weight of the book in our hands, the smell of coffee somewhere nearby, the sounds of a conversation in the next room that we know we shouldn't be listening to, but which evolution has taught us we can't completely ignore. It is all being taken in, but it isn't all immediately written to our internal hard drive. Instead, it is sorted in various interesting ways, given degrees of importance, and only what we really need to remember is transferred to our long-term memory in a process known as "consolidation." If we suffer a system crash before consolidation can take place, we don't remember any of it. Which in the case of a person involved in a painful car crash is a good thing.

Once a way to directly influence memory in a measurable way was found, the hunt was on to find a way to improve it so that we could learn quicker. Much of this early work was done with rats learning how to negotiate a maze. If their memory was improved, they would learn quicker. It wasn't long before

McGaugh discovered that if you gave rats a very small dose of strychnine (a poison in large doses, but a nerve stimulant in small doses), they would in fact learn quicker. But that didn't explain how it helped them learn. It was, after all, a nerve stimulant. Maybe it was increasing their sensitivity. Maybe they could run the maze quicker because they had a better sense of smell and so more easily located the cheese at the end of the maze. Maybe it had nothing to do with memory at all. And being rats, you couldn't ask them how they were doing it.

Which is where Dr. McGaugh made his first major discovery. He reasoned that what might be being affected was the consolidation of memory. What would happen if he gave the rats the stimulant not before they ran the maze but afterward? It seemed illogical that you could improve learning after it had happened—a violation of cause and effect—so illogical that his faculty supervisor thought the experiment would be a total waste of time and told him not to do it. But McGaugh couldn't stop wondering, so he waited until his boss went on sabbatical and ran the experiment while he was away. It worked, but only if the stimulation happened right after the learning. Wait too long and it had no effect. Stimulation clearly affected memory consolidation.

But stimulation of what? To answer that question, McGaugh and his associates began to apply small doses of stimulants to various areas of the brain and discovered that the key was not in the outer layer of the brain where the memories are eventually stored—the cerebral cortex—but in two small areas near the very center of the brain known as the basal amygdala. We have one of these small almond-sized ganglia on both the left and right sides of our brain. They are the areas that are most connected to all the rest of our brain, like a central switching station. The theory, which is strongly confirmed by experiments, is that when this area is stimulated, it sends out a "print that thought" notice to the rest of the brain and whatever is happening gets written in bold in our memory. Those moments become part of our mental map of the world.

A young child is told by his mother that the stove is hot, touches the stove before she can get to him, and receives a painful burn. Luckily, it isn't severe, but it does stimulate his amygdala to send out a "this is important" message, and that moment is engraved in memory and won't need to be repeated over and over again. The child has learned what "hot" means and that the stove is not to be touched. Now, so far this could be viewed as conditioned response—not that different from a dog that is conditioned to associate a bell with the arrival of dinner and so begins to salivate when a bell rings. The child associates hot with a burn and is conditioned to avoid the experience. Except that human beings are far more complex than dogs or rats, and that most of our learning doesn't involve physical pain. In fact, as cognitive psychology has shown, learning is inherently pleasant. So what is going on?

In 1975, McGaugh and his then postgraduate student Paul Gold made his second great breakthrough (and the one we are most concerned with here) by asking several basic questions: "Why are we designed by evolution to have a long period of consolidation? Why are we waiting to actually form our memories? Why don't we create them instantly?" It must have something to do with a chemical reaction because strychnine increases the amygdala's ability to create and consolidate memories. Rats don't produce strychnine, so what is that chemical mimicking? Whatever it is, it has to be important enough that evolution has designed us to wait for it. Given how central it is to our brains, it needs to be a matter of survival.

The answer was easy to find once they got the questions right. It is adrenaline, or its neurotransmitter cousin norepinephrine, which the stress hormone releases in the brain. When you get stressed, you remember better. Now it starts to make sense. One of our early ancestors is walking through the forest and sees a tiger come out of a cave up ahead. His body floods with adrenaline preparing for flight or fight. Since he is one of our ancestors and lived long enough to pass on his genes, he wisely chooses flight. As he sits behind a rock trying to catch his breath, he has plenty of time to mull over the experience as his amygdala, stimulated by the adrenaline, screams to the rest of his brain, "Remember that cave!"

To underline this connection between emotions and memory, Dr. McGaugh ran a brief experiment when we visited him at his lab in preparation for this book. He turned to one of us and asked, "Are you a writer?" After learning that his subject was emotionally invested in that skill set, McGaugh looked him right in the eyes and said, "Really? I've read some of your stuff. You know, it really is not very good. In fact, it stinks!"

He waited a moment then continued with a twinkle, "So, right now your heart is racing, your face is getting flushed, and you feel hot as your capillaries expand and you prepare for either fight or flight. That is the adrenaline entering your bloodstream. And whatever else you might remember from our conversation today, you will definitely remember the insult." He was right, both about the physical reactions and about our memories. That moment stands out clearly.

McGaugh uses this demonstration when he talks with the press, which, as one of the world's leading experts on memory, he does often. He told us that he had used it on a very well-known television journalist for a network show. She had the same reaction—flush, racing heart rate, increased memory of the moment. She loved it, and she knew that seeing it would make her audience remember the interview. Unfortunately, the camera had been focused on Dr. McGaugh as he spoke, so her reaction wasn't on film. She asked him to repeat what he said once her cameraman had shifted the camera position to get the reaction shot. McGaugh explained it wouldn't work. The strength of the adrenaline rush was determined by the intensity of the statement. Now that she was expecting him to insult her interviewing skills, it wouldn't work. He patiently waited for the cameraman to change the camera angle, then leaned in close and very sweetly said, "You know, you really should do something about your body odor. I heard some of your crew talking about it and they are really offended." The cameraman got the reaction shot, and she left with two unforgettable moments.

There are two things important to remember from this story. One, intensity of the emotion determines the amount of adrenaline released. That is one reason that McGaugh focused his attention on only one of us in our meeting—making it personal increased the intensity—and it is one reason why, when you want your points to be remembered, you shouldn't try to wow the whole room, but should focus instead on a few key listeners whose emotional reactions you can monitor. These will be the carriers of your message. They don't need to be the actual decision makers. Second, surprise is necessary—the more surprising, the more adrenaline. Which is why almost everyone can tell you where they were and what they were doing when they first heard about the events of 9/11. They remember that moment in much more detail than the rest of the day that surrounds it. Not just where they were, but how the air around them felt, the tone of voice of the person telling them, how their heart felt as they took in the words and made sense of what was being said. The almost dizzy quality of the moment as something inside them shifted. The shock that it could happen, plus the intense empathetic reaction of loss, was for many almost overwhelming. Adrenaline poured into the nation's collective bloodstream, marking that moment permanently, in many cases down to the smallest detail. Our bodies knew that we needed to remember that moment in order to survive.

Of course, insulting a client or threatening his life so that he remembers your talking points is probably not a sustainable communication strategy. But fear and suffering aren't the only things that trigger adrenaline. Pretty much anything that makes your heart beat faster will do it. Winning a sporting contest, your first kiss, your marriage vows—all produce strong emotions, and all are memorable, and they all will work. But memory is not emotionally neutral. There seems to be a bias toward negative, painful emotions. The experts aren't totally sure why. One reason might be that positive emotions are harder to access. What makes you glow with joy is very personal. Anyone gets angry when you tell them they stink. One of the reasons a good story often needs a good antagonist is to draw precisely those negative emotions away from your hero, whom your audience or client is already identified with. That way you have the emotion, and the memory, without alienating anyone.

But there are powerful positive emotions that almost everyone shares as well. We all like to win. And we like it even more when right after winning all of our friends get together and tell us just how wonderful we are. Remind you of anything? Well, not just *Star Wars,* but hundreds of other movie endings also. *Rocky. The Longest Yard.* The list is almost endless. Given the right sound track and the ability to focus on key moments and players, the director can create as much intensity as he needs, then all he has to do is give you a little bit of a surprise. You know Luke is going to win (he is the hero, after all), but you don't know exactly how, and when, after a little screenwriting sleight of hand, your judgment that the kid was a winner is confirmed, it is doubly pleasant. You will rush out of the theater with that moment engraved in your memory and the name *"Star Wars"* on the tip of your tongue.

It doesn't have to be an uplifting moment. In horror films, you often see the "Carrie ending." You think the film is over—the evil villain has been dispatched—and the camera moves in for a close-up and—snap—a hand comes shooting out of the grave and grabs the heroine by the leg. The best example of this we can remember is in the original *Friday the 13th.*

Having survived a night of incredible mayhem and bloodshed, the heroine is found floating safely in a boat in the middle of the lake as the sun mercifully rises above the haunted summer camp where all her friends have been brutally slain. The camera carefully lets us see there is no way she is in danger. The music playing is pastoral and relaxing (we are being given plenty of time for our already overstressed adrenal glands to recharge). Once we are finally, completely relaxed—WHAM! The demonic Jason comes shooting up from the depths of the lake, grabs our heroine, and pulls her under. Unlike the rest of this film, this last scene was edited by Wes Craven, one of the few real geniuses of horror. The timing is impeccable. We remember seeing it in Manhattan on Eighty-sixth Street. When the final shock hit, three tough-looking teens—any of whom we would have avoided in a dark alley—bolted from their seats and ran in full panic out of the theater. Moments later, we passed them on the street corner. They were laughing and telling anyone they could get to listen about what a great film they had just seen. One side effect of adrenaline is that it makes you talk fast and loud. *Friday the 13th* went on to have ten sequels (and still counting), largely based on the strength of that one moment.

Love stories can have the same effect. Many studies have shown that the most remembered line in all of film is "Frankly, my dear, I don't give a damn!" from *Gone with the Wind*. This works because it comes at the end of the film, is the culmination of a long and very emotional relationship, and "damn," though mild by contemporary standards, was totally surprising and very shocking in 1939. As a result, in constant dollar terms—actual tickets sold, actual eyeballs on the screen—*Gone with the Wind* is hands down the all-time box office champ.

Making memorable moments is particularly important in the film business. There is a saying that the star gets you the opening weekend, but it is the last ten minutes of the film that make it a hit. The first wave of audience comes to the film because they know the star and know what sort of films he is likely to be in. They like the star's brand and are already fans. But what makes a hit is word of mouth, and word of mouth is built in the last ten minutes of a film because that is the part the audience remembers as they walk out of the theater. That is why the last ten minutes of movies are constructed for maximum emotion.

So one key to making sure your presentation is remembered is making it emotional. But in business, many people feel that you shouldn't show any emotions at all. You should lead with your head, not your heart. This despite the fact that in a recent poll 92 percent of CEOs said that "customer satisfaction" was the next major area of corporate competition they were focusing on. Satisfaction is, after all, an emotion, so trying to provide it without discussing it or letting your salespeople express it seems counterproductive.

At the core of this prejudice against emotions is the idea that emotions somehow cloud business judgments. They don't. In fact, they are crucial to the decision-making process. In a series of tests with patients who have suffered brain injuries or lobotomies, and so are unable to experience normal emotions, it was found that not having emotions makes decision making very difficult. There was one exception. You can still play the stock market. But even there the tendency to herd reactions, the "irrational exuberance" that Alan Greenspan famously warned against as the stock market headed into the Tech Bubble of 2000, is an emotional phenomenon. If you ever actually go and stand on the trading floor—or in the gallery above it—the lingering stench of panicked flop-sweat and fried adrenal glands is unmistakable.

But the biggest reason you can't do a presentation without emotion is that human beings simply aren't wired that way. In a series of experiments done at University College London, Dr. Sophie Scott used a brain-scanning technique known as fMRI (functional magnetic resonance imaging) to show that when a person is listening to human speech, she is actually dividing the experience and remembering it in different parts of her brain. The words themselves (their syntactical meanings) are shuttled off to the left temporal lobe for processing, but the "melody" (the sound, intonation, and rhythm) is sent to the right side of the brain, a region more associated not only with music but also with spatial and visual images. We need to remember both sets of information because it is intonation and melody that often determine meaning. A friend can say, "Yeah, right," and mean they agree with us, they sarcastically disagree with us, or that they are too busy to give it any thought at all. Divorcing data from emotions often makes both meaningless. Even though we separate out melody from the words and send them to different parts of our brain for data processing, our memory is quite adept at keeping them linked. And that brings us to the second important thing about our memories—they are holistic.

The connection among memory, emotion, and language is exploited anytime we use a cleverly constructed acronym. Acronyms are names for organizations or programs that turn an idea into a simple, easily pronounceable word. When you can say it, the sound of your voice reinforces it powerfully in memory. The very best acronyms use a word that connotes an emotion the organization wants to elicit and harness. If you have kids in school, or attended school in the last twenty years, you probably know about the DARE program. DARE sends police officers into school classrooms and teaches kids to resist peer pressure that might lead them to take dangerous drugs. DARE stands for "Drug Abuse Resistance Education," and though there are many programs like it, it is by far the most widespread with over 36 million students involved worldwide and 26 million in DARE programs in the United States alone. Having an easily memorable name is one reason. A name that fits into one of its key slogans: "Dare to say no to drugs." Daring to do something, having the courage to say what you really feel, is the response you want kids to have in the emotionally charged environment of the playground when someone offers them a joint. Linking the organization to an easily remembered and emotionally appropriate word makes the name—and all the stories those police officers tell the kids that are associated with the DARE brand—hard to forget. If I am a school administrator looking for a program to help my students, the name "DARE" will just pop into my mind.

Another good example of this type of memory management is MADD (Mothers Against Drunk Driving), which plugs into women's anger at drunks on the road, and the same sorts of connections are used by NOW (the National Organization for Women), which seeks to harness women's impatience with the slow pace of political change to further its political agenda and raise funds. Later in this book, we will be using an emotionally charged visual image linked to a surprisingly appropriate acronym to help you remember our five-element story model.

Knowing that memory and emotion are inextricably tied, you can help your client by providing a clear context for the information you want remembered so that it is presorted and easier to absorb. That is another advantage stories have. We all understand the basic structure of stories so well that when you tell one it easily fits into your listener's memory in a way even the best PowerPoint presentation rarely can.

We all intuitively know that stories have heroes, and we are looking for one as we listen. When the hero arrives, we quickly file him or her away in the right place in our brain and then wait for the villain or obstacle to show up—they usually arrive in that order. After that, we can focus on how the hero will prevail and what awareness we are going to learn vicariously. That awareness is the real payoff. If a story produces no awareness, it will have no value—but we will deal with that in a later chapter.

When you work to have emotions in your presentation, be sure they are your real, authentic emotions. Don't try to create your emotions. It doesn't work. Just let them show through. Human beings are very good at understanding emotions, and even better at picking up on when they are being faked. If they were easy to fake, movie stars wouldn't get the million-dollar paychecks that they actually deserve.

As important as tone of voice and emotion are to memory, they aren't the only way to lock in a story. The more fully we engage the audience's entire brain in what we say—the more we get them firing on all cylinders—the more easy our story is to remember. Words and verbal constructions tend to be stored in the left hemisphere of the brain, spatial relationships and visual images in the right hemisphere (for those neuroscientists out there, we know we are vastly oversimplifying; and for the rest, hang in there, because we are getting to some very slick memory tricks).

Every year since 1991, memory mavens from around the world have come together for the World Memory Championships. In 2006, it was held at the Examination Schools at Oxford University. There, national champions competed in rounds that required them to accurately remember such things as a list of random words, the correct order of five decks of shuffled playing cards, an unfamiliar poem, and the faces of a group of people they had never met. The final, and most dramatic, event is Speed Cards. Contestants are given a single shuffled deck of cards and asked to memorize the order. As soon as they have done that, they hit a timer button to record how long it took them. Five minutes later, they will have to place a fresh deck of cards in that same order. No one has ever performed that memory feat in less than 30 seconds. That remains the equivalent of running a four-minute mile. But they are getting close. The 2006 winner was Kathenina Bunk, a fourteen-year-old German schoolgirl who memorized the deck in 45.6 seconds. How was she able to do it? By harnessing the emotional power of story.

At the level of world competition, most contestants use more or less the same method. They memorize the cards three at a time. Before the contest, they have assigned every card a person, an action, and an object. For example, the ace of spades might be Johnnie Cochran (a person) waving a sword (an action) at a police car (an object). The queen of diamonds might be Ivana Trump kissing a frog. And the Mike Tyson singing a lullaby to a crying baby is the jack of clubs. The more emotionally resonant those images are, the easier this is going to be. If I find the card sequence ace of spades, queen of diamonds, and jack of clubs in the deck, I combine the person from the first card, the action from the second, and the object from the third to make a sentence. The result is "Johnnie Cochran is kissing a crying baby," which is itself a visual image. To string that together with the other groups of three in the deck, I might imagine myself leaving the card images at places I routinely walk past on my way to work. To remember the right order, I later imagine myself retracing my morning walk and collecting the images I left there five minutes before. The more powerfully evocative my images, the easier it is to remember.

You'll notice that each of these images in fact meets our definition of a story—it is a fact, wrapped in an emotion that leads to an awareness (of what card comes where) that transforms the contestant's world, hopefully letting her win.

So when you are trying to make someone remember your persuasive argument, make it as visual as possible. Making the visual elements highly emotive gives you a double whammy; and if they are a little surprising or bizarre, that is even better. And linking them together in a formally remembered context like a story (the equivalent of that walk we have taken many times before) is the icing on the cake.

Most of the time that we are trying to persuade someone, we are either doing it in person so we can "close the deal" before they forget what they have been persuaded of, or we leave behind a paper version of our pitch to reinforce our client's memory. But there are two places where we can't, and where memory management is even more crucial: in the voting booth and in the jury room.

The bias of memory toward negative emotions (because they are more easily triggered when you don't know exactly whom you are talking to) is one reason why negative political ads are so effective. In the days right before the election, when everyone is desperately taking one last shot at persuading us of their position, these ads clog the airwaves. When they work, you can't get them out of your head, even though they are annoying. The ones that just list negative facts are easily countered by ads from the other side with other negative facts and end up being a wash. The mud doesn't stick. But the best ones, the ones we actually remember as we are casting our ballot (and which may have helped us to remember to go and vote in the first place), are emotional, visual, and fit into an already established context about the candidate they target.

Who can forget the jail cell door swinging open as Michael Dukakis let rapist Willie Horton go free to prey on our unsuspecting daughters, or John Kerry windsurfing this way and that as he cavalierly flip-flopped back and forth on all the important issues? Those ads did work. The most effective of the negative political ads is generally considered to be "Daisy," an ad run by the Lyndon Johnson campaign in his landslide victory over Barry Goldwater in 1964.

It begins with a beautiful young girl, the image of innocence, in a field of daisies. The camera moves toward her as she picks the petals off one of the flowers, counting as she does: "One . . . two . . . three . . . four . . ." As she stumbles over the number "seven"—she is very young—we focus in on her face, zooming in so that when she reaches "ten" we are tight on the black iris of her eye, which fills the screen. Now we hear another voice, this one counting down from ten: "Ten . . . nine . . . eight . . . " It is one of the most feared voices of the sixties—the cold professional voice of an Air Force officer counting down to a missile launch. When the count reaches "one," we see first the nuclear explosion, then the mushroom cloud, and then a blinding firestorm of light. We hear Lyndon Johnson's distinctive East Texas drawl paraphrasing W. H.

Auden, "These are the stakes: to make a world in which all of God's children can live, or to go into the dark. We must love each other, or we must die." An announcer's voice reinforces the point "Vote for President Johnson on November 3. The stakes are too high to stay at home." The firestorm fades to black and on that black card appear the words "Vote for President Johnson on November 3."

Senator Eugene McCarthy, who knew a thing or two about what makes you lose an election, called the Daisy ad "the most effective media campaign in American history." The ad ran only once—on September 7, 1964—during a run-of-the-mill movie of the week. At least, it only ran as an ad once. When the Republican Party realized how badly damaging the ad was and cried foul, every news show had to deal with it, and they were happy to. It is great television—a completely compelling thirty-second horror story with a morally strong uplift for a close. *Time* magazine put the ad on its cover. You couldn't forget it; the country couldn't stop talking about it.

It certainly meets our criteria of being hypermemorable persuasion. It is emotional—who doesn't love innocent little girls—and it is powerfully and simply visual, but where is the context? People are still screaming that this is the most negative of all negative campaign ads, yet it never actually even mentions Barry Goldwater.

It doesn't have to. Goldwater, who was a brigadier general in the Air National Guard, was an avid pilot and liked to be photographed in his flight suit climbing into his fighter plane. Good macho stuff, normally. Flying a fighter to defend your country isn't the same thing as launching a preemptive missile strike that will end the world, but it is close enough. That visual image of Goldwater as Air Force Warrior connected in our memory with the ad and left little doubt about whose voice it was giving that countdown to Armageddon. This impression was reinforced with a simple rhyming mnemonic, probably written by an unheralded copywriter at a Democratic ad agency, that swept the nation. Goldwater's campaign slogan was "In your heart you know he's right." Democratic wags replaced that with "In your guts, you know he's nuts." The joke stuck, and Goldwater was finished. After this ad, he never stood a chance.

But we don't consider this a purely negative campaign ad in the way, say, the Swift Boating of John Kerry was purely negative, and that is one reason it was so effective. You can't win an election by convincing people not to vote (though closing the polls early or jamming the voting machines in selected districts does help). Even if you aren't going to vote for Goldwater, it doesn't mean you are going to vote for Johnson. You could just not vote. But the end of this ad, which is often ignored in the analysis, doesn't focus on the problem to be overcome (nuclear war), but rather on the role of the hero in overcoming it. It makes it clear that it is a moral choice we are making. We are all "God's children" and "we must love each other or we must die." The ad enlists us into a just and deeply spiritualized struggle. When you put it that way, what choice do we have? We are drawn to the polls not to avoid the bad, but because we are inevitably drawn to supporting the good. It is that attraction to the good that really is our deepest emotional nature.

* * *

Linking into that commitment to doing the right thing is what trial lawyers know how to do best. And no one ever did it better than Johnnie Cochran during his summation at the O. J. Simpson trial.

In a national NBC poll done in 1999, the trial of former football great O. J. Simpson for the murder of his ex-wife Nicole Brown Simpson and her friend, Ronald Goldman, was voted the trial of the century, easily trouncing the second-place Nuremberg Trials of the Nazi war criminals. It has also been called "a great trash novel come to life." It is estimated that 91 million people watched at least some of the famous slow-speed car chase that led to Simpson's arrest. When the jury's verdict was announced live on TV, it was being watched by almost 150 million—a stunning 91 percent of all the people watching the tube at the time. The trial so captured the imagination of the public that when Boris Yeltsin came off the plane for a summit meeting with President Clinton, the first thing he said was, "So, do you think O.J. did it?" Everyone it seemed had an opinion. But only the opinion of the twelve jurors really counted.

Put yourself in their shoes as they are about to enter the jury room. You have just gone through the longest criminal court case in California history. You have heard 133 days of testimony. The prosecution alone called seventy-two witnesses. Much of the testimony was highly technical, dealing with DNA evidence in a pre-*CSI* world when that was still exotic. Some of it, like the recording of Nicole's earlier phone call to 911 pleading with police to send someone to keep O.J. from breaking into her house and beating her, was painfully emotional. And there were plenty of surprises and plot twists, including the prosecution's star witness being called to the stand by the defense and taking the fifth. Now, with the whole world watching, you have to make sense of this and come to a conclusion. Where do you start? Of all that information, what is important for you to remember? It is an almost superhuman task.

But you do have one thing going for you. Just before you went into the jury room, the prosecution and the defense had each summed up their case. Like all trials, it came down to a battle of stories.

The prosecution story was a classic. A jealous husband, confronted by evidence of his wife's infidelity (all right, ex-wife), snaps and brutally slashes her throat and the throat of the man he finds with her. Add the racial element of a black hero husband and a young, beautiful white wife and you are in *Othello* territory—one of Shakespeare's most produced plays and one many of us studied in high school. So the context of this story is well grooved in our brain. And the crime itself is visually compelling as we imagine in our minds the killer lunging from the shadows, grabbing the innocent victim from behind, killing her, and then fleeing into the night. We've seen it in hundreds of movies, to the point that it is almost a cliché. This story is bolstered by masses of forensic evidence. Much of it is technical, confusing, and in dispute by defense witnesses, but look at how much there was. Ninety-nine days' worth! So Assistant District Attorney Marcia Clark can close the case by telling the jury to just do the right thing. Look at the mountain of evidence and join the forces of justice in keeping women everywhere safe from abusive husbands.

It is a compelling story with all our elements. When the prosecution rested, Marcia Clark clearly felt she had won the case. If she seemed just a little bit smug, who could blame her? It had been a long, hard trial.

The story Johnnie Cochran had to sell the jury was much more complex—an elaborate conspiracy theory in which the LAPD was framing an innocent man for a crime they were not really interested in solving. The villain in this story wasn't a crazed husband, but Mark Fuhrman, a rogue racist police detective who would stop at nothing to frame and destroy a rich and successful black man who had dared to have a beautiful white wife. For the jury to buy this story, they had to ignore the mountain of evidence and focus on just those pieces that Cochran could use to bolster his case. The biggest piece for him was the famous bloody glove.

This was the blood-soaked glove that Detective Mark Fuhrman claimed to have found not at the murder scene, but behind O. J. Simpson's house miles away. The bloody glove never really made a lot of sense. O.J. kills his wife, wearing gloves, takes one off and leaves it at the crime scene, then travels across town and leaves the other under a plant at his house. The prosecution had a somewhat logical explanation for this timeline, but it was at best a little hinky. In and of itself the glove wasn't really that essential to the prosecution's case. But it was central to one of the trial's most embarrassing moments.

Egged on by Johnnie Cochran, Christopher Darden, a handsome and personable black assistant DA (and rising star in the District Attorney's Office), asked O. J. Simpson to put on the bloody glove used during the murder. What he was going for was an unforgettable visual moment—O. J. Simpson in the glove holding a knife. But it didn't work out. Either because the drying of the blood had shrunk the glove, or because Simpson was wearing a latex glove that protected the evidence and made his hand just slightly larger, or because he had spent the night before smashing his hand so that it was swollen (all three theories have been floated), the glove wouldn't go on his hand. It didn't fit. And at that moment Darden's career as a prosecutor went down in flames. The jury, predominantly made up of older African American women, liked Darden and had to empathize with his intense embarrassment. It would have broken any mother's heart.

Cochran captured that moment in a catchphrase: "If it doesn't fit, you must acquit!" He used that phrase over and over as he went through each piece of prosecution evidence, dismissing its importance or questioning its truth. He did a lot of other things right—he made sure his story had an innocent hero and a villain (he went so far as to compare Fuhrman to Adolf Hitler), and he enlisted the jury in the noble cause of stopping genocide—but it was the mnemonic device of a rhyming phrase recalling the most emotionally charged moment that the jury had in common that really did the trick. If the jury dived into that mountain of evidence and began to sort through it, Cochran knew he had lost; but if all they remembered was that bloody glove, he had won.

After a trial of eight months, the jury deliberation took just three hours (and according to later accounts, much of that time was just talking over how much they would miss each other when they were no longer sequestered together). O. J. Simpson was found not guilty.

Whether O. J. Simpson murdered his wife, or whether he was framed (or whether he murdered his wife *and* was framed, which is our favorite theory—though we freely admit that's just because for us it makes a better story), isn't the point. Our point is that Cochran used all of the factors needed to lock his story in his audience's memory—context, visual reinforcement, verbal cueing, and powerful emotions—and persuade the jury that it was his story—and only his story—they needed to remember.

What do we want you to remember from this chapter?

1. Emotions are crucial to memory, and memory is the basis of most business decisions.
2. The sound of your voice and the look on your face convey your emotions much more powerfully than the content of your words, and people can't really separate the two because they are stored together in memory. The more fully you engage the entire brain of your listeners, the more likely you are to be remembered. Memory is holistic.
3. The type of memory you need in business is almost always anchored in narrative. You can memorize a phone number by constant repetition, but is easier to just get a PDA. To be successful in business, it is emotional memories that really matter.

4. Visual elements and verbal repetitions are powerful mnemonic devices, and you should use them whenever possible.

5. Context is king. We remember things better if we can associate them with things and patterns we already remember from the past, if they fall along mental pathways we are used to traveling. The most powerful and central pattern our minds have is the storytelling elements—passion, hero, antagonist, awareness, and transformation. Whatever you do, don't forget to use them.

One common problem that storytellers face in the business world is that we are all trained to suppress our emotions. There are plenty of times it is necessary. We've certainly sat through meetings where we have had to bite our tongues. But emotional flexibility is a use-it-or-lose-it proposition. It is like physical flexibility—it requires a certain amount of regular exercise. Otherwise, your expression of the emotions in your story might seem so stilted that they are barely noticed, or so clumsy and overamped that they come across as hysterical and inappropriate. Hitting the right balance takes practice. Here is what we recommend.

For human beings, the voice, particularly the tone of voice, is the primary conveyor of emotion. Vocal training is a whole art in and of itself, but it is easy to start. Just start singing. Sing in the shower first—the tile surfaces give your voice good reverb and the warm water helps relax the muscles of your neck and chest. Keep your breathing deep, your diaphragm relaxed, your throat open, and, above all, enjoy yourself. Remember how much fun singing was when you were a kid? It still is that much fun; let yourself thoroughly enjoy it. And sing all sorts of songs. Sappy love songs. Rollicking drinking songs. Patriotic anthems. Rock and roll. Religious hymns. Faux Italian opera. You're alone in the shower. Go where your heart wants to go, wherever the melody leads you. Just go all the way.

When you think you are ready, take it to the next step. This one is a little scary, so bring along some good friends for emotional support. Go to a karaoke bar and get on stage and sing. You are going to feel really awkward and nervous at first. That is the adrenaline hitting your bloodstream. Flight or fight. It is what you want to feel. Now harness that emotional energy and channel it into the song to release the other more subtle emotions the song's story contains. Make it a song you've practiced in the shower, one whose words you know so you can focus on how the singing is making you feel. And remain aware of how the audience is feeling in response. After you have done this a few times, getting up and saying how you really feel about your boss's pet idea gets much easier. There is a reason that karaoke comes out of the highly stratified hierarchical world of Japanese corporate life. It is good executive training.

CHAPTER SEVEN

First You Invent the Disease

The favorite show at our house is *House*—the hour-long hospital drama starring Hugh Laurie as Gregory House, MD, a brilliant but wretchedly misanthropic medical Sherlock Holmes. If you haven't seen it, do yourself a favor and tune in to Fox to catch an episode or two. Or order the DVD of the first season (it is currently on its third and going strong). If you prefer to download your entertainment, the episodes you want to be sure to snag are the pilot and "Three Stories" from the first season. The creator of the show, David Shore, won an Emmy for that one. You won't be sorry you took the time to watch.

How can you not like a show that is so cuttingly true to emotional realities of life in the modern American workplace that the hero's boss—Dr. Cuddy, the female medical head of the hospital—can say to him, "Oh, I know this part. This is where you do something to make my life miserable, then I do something to make your life miserable. It is kind of fun because I'm always going to win. I have a head start. You are already miserable!"

And House is miserable. He is in constant pain—the result of a medical mistake that has left him with a bad limp and a need to gobble pain pills like junior high kids chew Tic Tacs. Though he is the mentor for a racially and gender-balanced team of three young and very attractive doctors—this is network TV, so most of the people we meet will be young and very attractive—he is a gleefully abusive boss. If he took his attitude down a few notches, his people skills would hover at brutally sarcastic, but as it is his crude and casual cruelty often makes us cringe. He is narcissistic, obsessive, and even lazy—refusing to get involved with real medical emergencies and instead hiding out in the rooms of comatose patients and watching hospital soap operas on TV! He rarely actually meets with his patients, and when he does he is either frightening them into taking some horribly painful and intrusive test, or being a bully out of force of habit. His view of the world, which is clearly stated in almost every episode, is "Everyone lies. The only variable is about what." That is not a point of view most of us want to share.

And yet he is the show's hero! True, we say that your stories should have a hero with a few imperfections so the audience can more easily relate to him or her, but Gregory House seems to be pushing that principle too far. And yet as a show and as a hero, House works. *House* has won its time slot since it premiered in 2004 and has an increasingly loyal fan base that collects and shares his nasty bon mots on the Internet, and in 2005 Hugh Laurie won the Golden Globe award—largely considered a popularity contest in Hollywood—for a character that shouldn't be popular at all. What gives?

One reason *House* is successful is that as bad as House's behavior is, what he is fighting against—his antagonist—is so much worse that we will always forgive him and take his side.

Week after week, House is up against an obscure and very nasty disease. It usually strikes someone attractive (network TV, remember); it is almost always fatal; it is always getting rapidly worse. We meet each week's antagonist—the disease—in the first scene when House's future patient first comes down with the symptoms. The symptoms are graphic, frightening, and quite often disgusting. A teacher begins to speak nonsense to her class of second graders, then collapses in front of the terrified children in a seizure. The seat of a young boy's pants is suddenly covered in blood as he experiences explosive, bloody diarrhea. In one of the series' visual signatures, we often go into the victim's body—moving along the bloodstream or through the neural pathways of the brain—so that we can actually see the physical damage the disease is doing up close and very, very personal.

Once we have met the enemy, then we are ready to join House in what, despite all his personal flaws, is always a noble fight. That is what a good antagonist does. It helps you get the audience emotionally committed to your cause.

* * *

The antagonist is the third of our five story elements. The antagonist is what is keeping your hero from achieving his or her goal. If we understand the antagonist, we understand the story. In fiction, it is usually personified as a villain, because what people understand most easily is other people, but *House* is proof that it doesn't have to be. If you are a doctor, your antagonist is a disease. If you are on the *Titanic*, your antagonist might be the sinking ship. If you're an airplane designer, it's air resistance. But your antagonist always requires your hero to take action and struggle. That struggle is going to need energy, and that energy is going to be released by our flight-or-fight response. Adrenaline is involved, so it will be an emotional process. We say that the antagonist corresponds to the element water because without a good antagonist your story will lack fluidity and movement, and that the antagonist is at the heart of your story because it is the interaction between the antagonist and the hero that releases your story's emotions.

As we saw in the last chapter, without emotions, your story won't be remembered, so you might as well save yourself the effort and not tell it; but even more, without emotions, your story won't matter enough for your client or customer to pay attention long enough for you to get to the point. Without the right antagonist, like House, he'll turn his attention to something else—office soap operas, mental video games, or plotting how to make his boss's life miserable. Give him the right antagonist and you'll not only have his attention, he'll be strongly rooting for you and joining you in fighting the good fight.

Luckily, as a storyteller, the antagonist is the element you have the most control over. In commercial storytelling, your passion—your motivation—is most often a given. You, your company, or your team are who you are. You can get your team tuned up, and you can choose the right corporate face, but you can't be all things to all people, and you shouldn't even try. That is a recipe for disaster. You *do* control what it is you are trying to do. You choose your goal and which obstacle is keeping you from reaching it at any given moment. How you define that obstacle—how well you and your team understand your antagonist—has a lot to do with whether you will succeed or fail. Choose the right "enemy" and you are more than halfway to winning. Choose the wrong one—or worse yet, be afraid to choose and remain unfocused—and you and your team's story will spiral inevitably toward defeat.

But be careful. The antagonist is the trigger for your story's emotions, and as every love-struck teenager knows, emotions easily get out of control and are often double-edged swords. But that isn't going to happen to you, or at least it is less likely to it if you keep reading. As Sun-tzu, who we mentioned before, says in his *Art of War,* "Know your enemy and know yourself and in a thousand battles you will be undefeated." So let's go and kick some butt—but first we have to figure out just whose butt it is we are going to kick.

And that is what House spends most of each episode doing. As he does it, he is going through each of our five story elements in sequence. We tune in and immediately meet a person we care about—a child, a teacher, a cop—who is struck down in his or her prime, and our common passion—our *compassion*—kicks in. We care. The show has our attention. After the credits, we immediately meet our heroes, House and his team, whose strengths and failings we already know from last week, and whose points of view we are comfortable assuming. Then, for the rest of the hour, we watch as House struggles to figure out just what he is really up against. If it were a common disease, House would know it in a minute and cure it quickly (actually, it would bore him and he would probably avoid the case, and we can't blame him, because if it were a common disease, we'd have changed the channel), but this week's antagonist is different. It is sneaky. It is rare and exotic. It seems to morph and change just before every commercial break. That cliffhanger moment dumps adrenaline into our bloodstreams and makes it more likely we'll remember the commercials that follow—and they are, after all, paying for this little emotional adventure of ours. This week's disease lurks inside a list of symptoms that don't make sense, or leave us with way too many mutually exclusive possibilities to take effective action (sound a little like your day at work?). It will take a doctor of a certain type of genius to find its name. But once it is named, like Rumpelstiltskin, it is defeated. Once House knows his antagonist, the cure is usually quick.

That flash of insight—that moment of awareness when House figures it out—usually comes as he runs all the information around in his head looking for a story line that fits. Often he is staring at a board on which the symptoms are listed as he twirls the cane that his own illness forces him to carry. It is a sign of just how good an actor Hugh Laurie is that we can actually see him thinking things through. He is literally taking the information into himself and wrestling with it. It is one of the key functions of the antagonist to let us internalize the story. The hero gives us a way into the story, but it is the antagonist that forces us to take it into ourselves and make it our own. Sometimes the answer comes to House when he sees a small, almost unnoticeable detail in the patient's behavior, or overhears some seemingly unrelated remark. However it comes, the answer is always a moment of pure inspiration.

After that the cure is quick, and the transformation complete, as the now-healthy patient walks out of the hospital, leaving House battling his own private demons and waiting until his gift is needed again next week. Passion, hero, great antagonist, moment of awareness, and a sick person is transformed into a healthy one. Five and out.

So one reason we tell our clients to watch *House* is that it proves our theory. We say, and cognitive psychology confirms, that human beings organize almost all of their experiences as stories, but there are stories and then there are stories. When you are looking at something as elusive and mercurial as the sources of human emotional response, it can help to study fictional stories, where things are more starkly black and white. We have all experienced jealousy. If you want to really understand it, read *Othello*.

There is another reason we suggest watching *House*. The medical world actually works like that. The major pharmaceutical firms—Big Pharma—have consistently been the leading market sector in terms of profits per share despite facing significant marketing obstacles. So if we understand how they do that—and more specifically, how they use the power of the antagonist to do it—we are well on our way to making a lot of money and winning our own marketing struggles.

It costs Big Pharma an average of twelve years in R & D and as much as $1.8 billion to roll out just one new wonder drug. Most of that money will be invested before there is any guarantee that the drug will work, so a few big winners have to finance all the losers. Even if your research team comes up with a winner, the window of opportunity for selling it is extremely short. Your patent is good for only about twenty years; after that, the generics will be on you like piranha. In fact, your own company might begin marketing a generic even before the patent expires to get a jump on this lucrative secondary market, shortening your period of maximum profitability even more. And there is always the very real possibility that as science marches on, another team of researchers will come up with a better drug before your twenty years are up and that this new drug will become the treatment of choice, leaving your firm, which was first into the market, out in the cold.

Add to this that there is no transfer of brand loyalty to the parent company (when I like my Mustang I am much more likely to buy a Ford next time; but when I use Lipitor, I don't care, or even necessarily know, that it is made by Pfizer), and that the name I choose for my new drug will probably be great for Scrabble but not easily remembered (all the easy ones are long gone), and it is easy to see why Big Pharma is not a game for the faint of heart.

But these companies do have a few things going for them. One, they are run by very smart people. Maybe the smartest—and certainly the best-educated—executives in the country. Just having one PhD rarely gets you a seat at the big table. And the demographics slant in their favor. As the country gets older, more and more people need what they have to sell. And every year new discoveries are making diseases that were incurable potential profit centers. But the biggest thing in their favor is their antagonist. Like House, they are fighting the right enemy, so we are all on their side and rooting for them. If I am sick—or even more, if my child or parent is sick—I will pay whatever I need to pay, do whatever I need to do, to make myself or them well. Emotionally, I can't do anything else. And it is emotions that drive actions—at least they will drive actions if they are properly focused. If they aren't focused, emotions can just as easily paralyze (fight or flight, right?). Focused on what? On the antagonist. But before I can really focus you so that you buy my new drug and defeat our mutual enemy, like House, I have to give that enemy a name. Big Pharma calls this process "inventing the disease."

Of course, the disease already exists. If they are talking to people that find that phrase a little too much like something Dr. Evil would say, they will refer to this process as "meeting the unseen need" or even more obscurely as "creating the lock and key," but the phrase they use most often among themselves is the one that is the most emotionally charged and so is the easiest to remember—inventing the disease. Inventing it where? In the minds of their main target audience—the physicians who write the prescriptions.

Physicians are deeply, emotionally committed to relieving pain and suffering. If they weren't, they wouldn't go through the grueling process they do to become doctors. So Big Pharma has their attention, but there are three main reasons why they might not prescribe a drug that would cure a disease.

- One, they might not see the disease as a disease at all, but as a natural part of the aging process. You can't cure getting old. The most you can do is treat the symptoms.
- Two, the physician might know that it is a disease, but if there is no cure, then he or she will put it out of mind as quickly as possible and move on. Triage— the art of sorting cases into those that can be fixed quickly and those that can't and setting priorities—is one of the first skills doctors learn on entering an ER as interns, and the Hippocratic oath teaches "First, do no harm." Doctors only have so much emotional energy. They have to pick and choose their battles. If there is no cure, don't dwell on it, move on. It is better for you. It is better for your patient. If you start fiddling around with too many tests, you might make things worse.
- Three, the patient might not know she is sick, or might be too embarrassed to tell her doctor the

details. This is one of the main things House means when he says, "Everyone lies." So part of inventing the disease is telling doctors what physical symptoms to be looking for that patients might not even know they have, and part of it is letting patients know it is all right to tell their doctor about the symptoms they do notice, that it isn't just whining. This is why the FCC now allows direct advertising of prescription drugs—as a means of educating the public so people can talk more openly with their doctors.

When a drug company gets ready to release a new drug, it is always facing a combination of these three problems; just the mix is different. When Amgen prepared to release Kineret, the first of a new class of drugs to treat rheumatoid arthritis, it mostly had to deal with a combination of problems one and two. People with arthritis talk about it because it hurts, and even if they don't, the swelling of the joints is obvious with simple observation, so problem three wasn't much of an issue. Doctors know that rheumatoid arthritis is a disease, but the situation is complicated by the fact that there are two very different types of arthritis. They both present similar symptoms. Osteoarthritis is by far the most common, with about 20 million sufferers. This type *is* a result of aging. Though there are some new treatments coming on line, most of what medicine has to offer these patients is pain relief. The other form of arthritis, rheumatoid arthritis, is a disease of the autoimmune system. For reasons we are just beginning to understand, the body attacks its own cartilage as if it were a foreign invader.

Only about 2.1 million people suffer from this, but the suffering is more intense and crippling. Because it is a disease in the more classic sense, a cure might be possible. When scientists discovered that one reason for the swelling caused by rheumatoid arthritis was the overproduction of a specific protein—interleukin-1—a team at Amgen began to develop a drug that would block this protein's effect. If it worked, it would be whole new way of directly attacking the disease, rather than just trying to suppress the pain. But because both osteoarthritis and rheumatoid arthritis have for years been thought to be incurable, doctors were lumping the two together and moving on without really finding out which form the patient had. Why bother with expensive tests if the treatment for both is the same—a pain pill? No matter how effective Amgen's new drug was in theory, if it didn't get into the hands of the people who needed it it couldn't help anyone. Amgen had to get almost two hundred thousand doctors to start seeing arthritis differently.

In sales, as in comedy, timing is everything (just ask Jack Benny, who was the best ever at selling a joke). If Amgen had begun actively reinventing the disease too early—talking up rheumatoid arthritis too far in advance of the approval of its new wonder drug—it would only increase everyone's sense of being powerless. But the whole point of reinventing the disease is to empower the physicians by showing them that here is an enemy that they can now defeat. So Amgen waited for the right moment and then funded a series of studies on the connection between rheumatoid arthritis and interleukin-1. It even published a glossy medical book and opened up a Web site with chat rooms dedicated to the subject. It wasn't that different from how you launch a film or a political campaign. In doing this, Amgen was defining the disease at the level where the company would most easily be seen as the victor in any contest. In the minds of the doctors reading the articles, arthritis was now becoming a molecular problem—a version of good molecules gone bad. And what do you use to fight a bad molecule? A good one, in the form of a wonder drug, Kineret (though Amgen wisely didn't actively push its own solution in the first salvo of papers, saving that for later).

This sort of corporately funded research has gotten controversial recently, but in this case Amgen didn't try to slant the data. It didn't need to. The company didn't interfere in any way. But it did coordinate the effort. How coordinated was it? Color coordinated. When you wrote in for a reprint of an article, or when you went on to the Web site, you were seeing the same colors that would be on the eventual packaging of Kineret once it was released. If Amgen were going to spend time and money defining the enemy, it was going to make it very easy for you to find the cure, even on crowded pharmacy shelves. Like we said, the people who run these companies are very smart.

About a year before the drug would become available Amgen began to more actively release the results of the tests that showed Kineret worked. It was not only building buzz—more important for the company's stock price than for physicians, really—but it was also establishing its credibility. These tests generate reams of data, mostly numbers. Doctors are trained to think critically, and if they don't get lots of numbers, they don't take you seriously. But numbers are just facts devoid of emotion, and we know that that is not enough. The numbers give doctors the intellectual permission to prescribe the drug; they won't give them an emotional reason to actually do it. For that, the information has to be more personal.

As Stalin once said, "One death is a tragedy, a million is a statistic." And statistics are, well, statistics. If I am really inventing the disease, I need to give my enemy a personal face. Choosing the right case studies does this. Not that many—three to five usually works. The drug tests might involve hundreds, even thousands, of patients. But as a doctor, I don't have hundreds of patients with rheumatoid arthritis. I have four or five. Give me clear examples of people who are like the people I see every day and I can internalize what you are telling me, remember it, and make it part of my practice. I'll start writing the prescriptions. All I ask is that you tell me real stories of how it helped real people. And, of course, that is just what Amgen did.

As a result of this effort, there was a renewed understanding of rheumatoid arthritis among physicians and a pool of pent-up demand was waiting for the release of Kineret, which quickly became very profitable. Maybe more important, it got into the hands of the people who needed it and began to relieve real human suffering. As an unexpected positive side effect, the drug is now showing promise in treating some of the effects of Alzheimer's. There are obvious ways that this system can be abused, but overall we believe it works. And clearly defining the antagonist is a big reason why it works. If Amgen hadn't done that, all that Kineret would be on a shelf someplace and people would still be hurting.

Of the problems we discussed—it not being a disease, it not having a cure, or it not being noticed and talked about—the one problem Amgen didn't face, or, at least, faced less than the others, was patients not telling their doctors about their disease. But in corporate storytelling, this is often the first and most pressing problem your antagonist will have to address.

Everyone lies, particularly to themselves. Clients and customers may not clearly know why they have a problem, and the anxiety they feel often resolves itself in denial that there is any problem at all. This goes double if you are bringing a project up the corporate ladder. There is usually strong institutional resistance to talking about real problems—careers and stock prices may be negatively impacted, and everyone fears having their name associated with failure. If there is a problem, it certainly isn't one that someone lower in the food chain might be able to see clearly and solve. Just defining the problem might be seen as threatening to people you need on your side.

In this situation, you are more like Pfizer when it discovered that the compound sildenafil, which was being tested as a possible treatment for angina, had the unexpected side effect of giving the male test subjects raging erections. Before they could market this drug under the name Viagra, they needed to reinvent male impotence as something red-blooded American men might, just might, admit was a problem.

How they did that and turned Viagra into one of the most successful drugs of the last ten years is a great case study in using the fluid nature of the antagonist. Like the diseases on *House,* your story's antagonist needs to be constantly changing and revealing new aspects of itself. This not only broadens your market, it also keeps your story emotionally fresh and alive. The one emotion you never want your audience to feel is boredom.

Sex is embarrassing. Even good sex with someone you love, if you look at it objectively, is a little goofy. Luckily for the continuation of our species, we don't usually look at it that way, instead surrounding it in a thick cocoon of our deepest and most heartfelt emotions. Emotions produce actions, but these emotions are so intense that they have to be addressed very, very delicately. And sex is one of the three things that surveys show most American males think they do better than average (the other two are driving a car and telling a joke). Since early adulthood, most males have spent time in groups bragging about their sexual exploits, but they are extremely reticent to discuss any sexual failures even with their most trusted friends, because if they did, the group would often laugh at and ridicule them. Viagra would be a prescription drug, so getting it would require a conversation with your doctor. Unlike arthritis or a heart murmur, male impotence doesn't have any external symptoms that show up in a normal exam. Unless you tell your doctor you have a problem, the condition remains hidden.

When asked at the end of the exam if there is anything else bothering them, most men will respond "No," not only because everyone lies, but also because in large part prior to Pfizer's campaign to reinvent the disease, most men didn't see impotence as a medical problem. They saw it as a deep personal failing. A personal failing that denial often converted into a personal choice ("I'm just not really in the mood, you know") or blamed on their partner for not "turning me on anymore," a situation that often resolved itself in the ultimate flight from emotional intimacy—silent, sullen anger. Pfizer needed to get American men in the mood to stand up and fight.

It is a fact that testosterone levels decrease with age and that male libido tends to follow. So a chemical solution to the problem seems logical. But there is very little that is logical about sex. Pfizer had its work cut out for it. It wouldn't be enough to convince two hundred thousand physicians that it had a potential cure; it would have to convince 100 million American males that if they did have a problem, talking about it would get them help, not laughed at.

The first thing Pfizer needed to do was change the name. Impotent means powerless. If you are powerless, you can't change, so why bother trying. The condition needed to be re-invented as "erectile dysfunction." Pfizer found the right corporate spokesman to help make the transition in Bob Dole. If impotence means powerlessness, then having one of the most powerful politicians in the country—he had just run for president of the United States, the "most powerful man in the world"—would show that erectile dysfunction wasn't that. During the 1996 presidential campaign, it had been frequently mentioned that Dole was a war hero, so his virility and courage were without question. And morally, he was above reproach. If he could suffer from this new erectile thing, anyone could.

Dole went on talk shows and on the *Today* show and talked very openly about it, which only proved his courage even more, because it was something most men were afraid to even think about, let alone admit to. The fact that he was being very well paid to do it only increased his image as a powerful winner. He wasn't on those shows whining about his problems like some trailer-trash loser; he was out there making money, and lots of it. What could be more red-blooded American than that? The fact that his right arm was not fully functional because of his war wound was always in the back of our minds when we saw him speak, adding just the right Freudian kick to his message. He was the perfect spokesman for this stage of Pfizer's pitch.

Because he was plainspoken with a gentle Kansas accent and a self-deprecating sense of humor, it seemed natural that he would refer to erectile dysfunction as the easier to say and much less threatening "ED." Like TB or MS, it is clearly a disease, so you would use a drug to fight it. But ED is also a name: Ed. And we all know an Ed. We probably know a few. We can all beat up Ed, if we really wanted to. If erectile dysfunction's name had been shortened to Bruno or Spike, maybe it would give us pause, but we sure can go and kick old Ed's ass. We just need to talk to our doctors first, then we will be on our way to a fight we are bound to win.

But getting me to see that I am not powerless to have a conversation with my doctor is not quite the same as getting me revved up to actually have it.

For that, Pfizer went to stage two, again redefining the enemy and making it more likely its target audience would take action. Everyone has sex, and everyone drives a car. But no one drives a car like a NASCAR driver. So sponsor a car and have a young, virile American hero climb in and out of it every week right past your product name written large on the fender. Viagra is no longer about curing a disease; it is about getting maximum performance.

Around this time, either through good fortune or design (we have no way of knowing which), a series of articles started appearing in newspapers that Viagra was being abused as a new sex drug. Kids were taking it at raves. Octogenarians were having orgies in their nursing homes. Goodness gracious, who knew what would happen next? Now, when you walk up to the pharmacist to get your prescription filled, you're not admitting to having a problem—maybe you are just a wild party animal out on the prowl. The market for Viagra has expanded beyond people in chronic need to people who might just want to a have a great date on their anniversary and really wow the missus by feeling like the guy they were twenty years ago. Nothing wrong with that. The men who use Viagra aren't broken, they aren't getting fixed—they're just getting a tune-up.

At this point, almost every male in America is either talking to his doctor about Viagra, or talking to his friends about how to score some on the sly, and sales on the Internet are beginning to spike.

The final redefinition of the antagonist that began as impotence and then became ED wasn't done by Pfizer—it was making plenty of money right where it was, thank you very much—but by a competitor, Eli Lilly. Its drug, Cialis, which works along different vectors to solve the same problem, is known as the weekend drug. Its effects are longer lasting, and it markets itself as "ready when you are." Its commercials show loving couples beginning to get intimate, then being interrupted by normal life—phone calls, friends arriving, grandkids coming over—but that's OK, because Cialis will still be active a few hours later when they will have time to express their love. The enemy now isn't being powerless, or even a lack of horsepower; it is the normal stressors of modern life. You're not taking Cialis because you're sick, or because you want to be a stud; you're taking it because you're a busy man who works long and hard, has a complex schedule, and it seems the polite thing to do. Impotence has gone from being a something you can't talk about to being something any responsible husband would think about as he plans his weekend. And along the way, everyone involved has made a lot of money.

In Viagra's case, none of this would have been possible without direct marketing to the end consumer, so now seems a good time to talk about one of the most distinctive elements of drug ads—the listing of the side effects.

It is true that this is required by the FDA, and many of these side effects are potentially life threatening, so the moral and ethical thing to do is to make sure people know about them, but the way they are mentioned in the ads—the emotional tone that surrounds their listing—is what sets drug ads apart. It is, for example, totally different from the ultraquick recitation of credit data that car companies are also required to include in their ads. Car companies just want to get past the bad news and move on quickly. Drug ads take the time to dwell on potential problems almost lovingly. The announcer's voice is warm and caring. Often a sympathetic authority figure looks us straight in the eye as he tells us about the potential for diarrhea, dizziness, or dry mouth. They do this because the drug companies are master marketers and understand that the function of an antagonist is to allow us to internalize their story line and make it part of our reality. And, of course, their product, a pill, is something we will have to physically internalize to make use of. If they let us see the problem, they let us join in the good fight.

We have every reason to not want to admit we have a problem with high blood pressure. Thinking about it actually increases our blood pressure. So we are emotionally primed to reject ads that discuss it and literally not to hear them. But we all have had diarrhea, and we've beaten it. It is already part of our life experience, so it is a word we hear clearly and take in. In fact, it is one we are almost compelled to listen to, particularly if we have had to deal with dirty diapers. Once we start listening to an ad, really letting the information in, the rest of the ad will follow right along. All the storyteller wants to do at that point is to get us to open up. Remember, whether the emotional reaction is positive or negative, as long as there is an emotional reaction the story is much more likely to be remembered and acted on. And if what the ad is warning us about is the necessity of immediately contacting a physician if we experience an erection that lasts for more than four hours? Well, for us, at that point, we are past just letting that information in; we are flat-out intrigued by it. Intellectually, we know that the condition being described—priapism—is serious and very painful. But we can't help it. Every time we hear that part of the ad, it makes us smile lasciviously. Which is, of course, exactly the emotional reaction Pfizer wants us to have whenever we think of the name "Viagra." Problems, properly used, become positives. The power of the antagonist.

We don't want to give the impression that medical stories somehow have a corner on good villains. They don't. (Though, come to think of it, Hannibal Lecter did have an MD.) *Every* good story needs a strong antagonist—and not just stories designed to market products. Finding the right antagonist is even more important for stories that companies tell themselves to coordinate their energies so they will have something to market in the first place. This is particularly true for small design teams—where speed of execution is crucial and the need to innovate is a given.

Lockheed's Skunk Works, one of the world's premier aircraft design firms, has developed many of the U.S. military's finest aircraft over the last sixty years. Their successes include the U-2 spy plane, the F-117 stealth fighter, and the SR-71 Blackbird, officially the world's fastest aircraft. (Unofficially, there are strong rumors that Skunk Works has an even faster plane hidden in the wings, ready to roll out when it is really needed.) Its black-budget projects are too numerous and secret to list. Compared with the thousand-plus engineer design teams now normal in the aerospace industry, Skunk Works is extremely small and nimble, and it is the only firm known for consistently coming in ahead of schedule and under budget. In fact, it routinely returns to the government money it didn't need to use—which really weirds the Pentagon out. A big reason for the intense loyalty and creative cohesion that Skunk Works is known for is expressed in its motto: "It takes a great enemy to make a great airplane."

What Skunk Works understands is that in a good corporate story (and it's the corporate story that defines corporate culture), conflict and struggle are far from destructive. Properly used, they can create a positive atmosphere for innovation. The right antagonist helps unify your team and keep it focused on a common goal by keeping everyone emotionally involved. Of course, Skunk Works had an advantage in coming to this realization. It hit the ground running with one of history's great villains already waiting for it: the Nazis.

In 1943, as General Dwight D. Eisenhower was preparing for D-Day, he began to hear rumors of a top secret plane Hitler was rushing into production. A plane that could fly almost six hundred miles per hour and didn't have propellers. The U.S. War Department had been approached years before about developing a jet engine but had rejected the idea. Now, if the United States didn't come up with something to counter this new Nazi fighter, the battle over the beaches of Normandy would go the wrong way and the invasion would be a disaster. So the Army Air Corps turned to its ace designer, Clarence "Kelly" Johnson, and asked him to design a whole new type of airplane, one that would fly almost 50 percent faster than anything the United States had at the time, and have it ready in just six months.

Johnson, a former dockworker, had designed the P-38,

the fastest plane in the U.S. arsenal, and in one forty-eight-hour marathon session had redesigned a Lockheed airliner to become the standby of Britain's bomber fleet, the Hudson. So when he got the new job, he knew just what to do. He bought a circus tent.

He set it up in the parking lot next to Lockheed headquarters in Burbank, and moved in his team of twenty-three engineers and thirty shop mechanics. One hundred forty-three days later, and over a month ahead of schedule, they had built America's first jet fighter, the XP-80, nicknamed *Lulu-Belle*.

Johnson kept his team together, and Skunk Works was born. In the process, he began to develop his famous 14 Rules, which are now widely studied and emulated in the aerospace industry. But it is one of his de facto rules that he always applied but isn't on that list that we find most interesting.

He felt strongly that designers should always be within a stone's throw of the plane they were designing. He wanted his people to be directly and physically involved in solving the problems of creating the aircraft. At one point, a labor dispute led to his machinists walking off the job. Without missing a beat, his design team jumped in and started lathing the pieces they needed themselves. He later said that this had actually made everyone work better. Not only did it shorten the schedule, because they no longer had to spend time explaining to another person what it was they wanted, it also fully engaged the designers in the physical creation of the plane and so allowed them to more fully feel the emotional satisfaction that came from a job well done. Getting his designers out of their heads and into their hearts so that they literally loved what they were doing was a big part of what made Skunk Works such a uniquely creative design shop.

And Kelly wasn't afraid to put himself in the situation of the people he was designing for. In Kelly's case, that meant fighter pilots. So he had to quite literally risk crashing and burning. An avid pilot himself, he said, "If I didn't get the hell scared out of me once a year, I wouldn't have the proper balance to design future aircraft." If he hadn't been willing to take that risk, things like wind shear and airflow stall vectors would have remained intellectual abstracts. But because he had lived through the terror of pushing the envelope just a little too far, he was fully and emotionally committed to solving the problems on the drawing board. Good enough wasn't going to be good enough for him. He knew the price that might eventually be paid. That sort of creative commitment is contagious. Skunk Works works because nothing brings people closer together than a common struggle. Again, the power of the antagonist.

So your story needs a good antagonist, and if you stop to see what is keeping you and your client or customer from reaching your goal, you will be able to define one in a way that releases the emotions you need to make your ideas memorable and that lets your listeners take the actions you want them to take. But be careful. As we mentioned before, emotions once released are hard to control and they can often act as double-edged swords. But if you are emotionally centered enough not to rush in before you are ready, you can see most of the problems in time to avoid them. There are two key things we always tell our clients to absolutely avoid.

1. *Don't create straw villains.* These are antagonists that you pull out of thin air, or puff up beyond the problems that they actually pose, to make your idea or product seem more important than it actually is. That sounds like it would be a good strategy, but the danger here is that once you have created these villains in the mind of your audience, they might actually become real. Sort of an instant-karma thing. A good example is the problem Merck is having with Vioxx. Vioxx is a good painkiller, but there were already plenty of good painkillers on the market when it was first released, and it wasn't that much better than ibuprofen. It did have one big advantage. It was easier on the stomach lining. If a patient took ibuprofen for a long time, particularly after surgery, it might produce a bleeding ulcer, and in a small number of cases, those ulcers might go undetected and people might bleed out—they might die before they could be properly treated. No doctor would want that, but as every episode of *House* makes clear, medicine is always a calculated risk. So Merck had to make the dangers of ibuprofen very personal to doctors in order to get their attention. Somehow—and we're not saying how (though Merck does have a lot of drug reps out there talking to a lot of people)—doctors got the idea that if

they prescribed the wrong drug—the less-expensive and common drug—and a patient died of an ulcer, they might end up being sued by evil trial lawyers who would claim the physician hadn't done everything in his or her power to protect the patient. It was a very slick trick. Vioxx was no longer a tool to fight pain; it was now a tool to fight malpractice. What doctor wouldn't want to sign up to fight that? Vioxx became wildly successful and, it is now commonly agreed, widely overprescribed. It also became Merck's major profit maker. A marketing miracle.

As we are sure you know, that isn't the end of the story. Vioxx has a nasty side effect that doesn't show up until lots and lots of people start taking it over an extended period of time. It increases the risk of heart attack. Once lots of people were doing just that, the problem surfaced, but Merck did just what its patients normally do when they first discover they have a problem—it went into denial. You would think its marketing gurus, who were so familiar with that problem, would have done something to wake up the rest of the corporate board, but they didn't. As a result, all of those nasty trial lawyers that had been conjured in the minds of the physicians became very, very real indeed. But the lawyers aren't suing the doctors; they are lining up to take Merck down. And they just might do it.

So when you're crafting your story's antagonist, be careful what you wish for. Keep your emotions in check, don't let things get overinflated, and be sure you keep it real.

2. *Don't demonize your antagonists so that you lose contact with them.* Mario Puzo had it right in *The Godfather*: "Keep your friends close, but your enemies closer." If you let your or your client's feelings against the antagonist progress all the way to animus, you will lose contact with the antagonist and your story will lose much of its forward drive. You will also lose the very real possibility that your antagonist has something to teach you. The whole point of the struggle is to eventually give your story's hero a moment of awareness that allows him to bring about real and positive change. That is what the Dalai Lama means when he says, "Some of my best teachers have been my enemies." If you lose contact with the antagonist, you won't learn those lessons. So while your hero is struggling with the villain, he is also always carefully listening to what the villain has to say. Even in situations where you think your opponent has nothing to say that would help, and that even if he did, he would certainly refuse to say it, he always has something to tell you. Even if it means he will stand trial for murder.

If there is ever a time an antagonist shouldn't be willing to tell the truth, it is when he is a suspect in a murder case. But Jerry Giorgio, the NYPD's legendary interrogator, says that isn't so. Famous for his ability to get even the most hardened gang members to confess, Giorgio is known on both sides of the law as "Big Daddy Uptown." Here is how he says he does it.

"Everybody knows the Good Cop/Bad Cop routine, right? Well, I'm always the Good Cop. I don't work with a Bad Cop either. Don't need to. You want to know the truth? The truth is—and this is important—everybody down deep wants to tell his or her story. No matter how damaging it is to them, no matter how important it is for them to keep quiet, they want to tell their story. If they feel guilty, they want to get it off their chest. If they feel justified in what they did, they want to explain themselves. I tell them I know what they did. They want to tell me about it, show remorse, I'll go to bat for them. If you give them half a reason to do it, they'll tell you everything."

Of course, it isn't quite that simple. They start talking and they start lying. Like House says, "Everybody lies." But Giorgio listens carefully to them, pointing out things they say that just don't quite make sense, and eventually the tangled web they are trying so hard to weave comes apart, revealing the truth inside. It is the same moment of awareness that House has every week as he struggles with the symptoms, but with Giorgio it is for real.

The people he is talking to have committed heinous crimes, and often he has seen the crime scene photos to prove it. His initial reaction is what any of ours would be—anger and disgust. But he doesn't let his personal emotions get in the way of a good story. Because he is emotionally flexible enough to maintain contact with the antagonist and still be open to listening and learning, he is eventually able to take the story where he needs it to go. If you can do the same thing, you will be fully harnessing the power of your story.

So, to sum up.

1. Every story, both factual and fictional, has an antagonist—something standing between the hero and his goal. It is the struggle to overcome the antagonist that gives the story its emotional power—and stories are facts wrapped in emotions. For those emotions to fully engage us, something has to be at stake—the life of a child, the safety of the free world, everyone's job. The choice is yours because defining the antagonist is one of the elements of the story that the storyteller is most in control of. Find the right antagonist and the right stakes and we will forgive your hero for almost anything. We'll be won over to your side of the fight.

2. When you are defining your antagonist, make sure

it is something that your hero can overcome. The function of the villain isn't to trap you in endless conflict, but rather to move the story toward a positive conclusion.

3. Our understanding of the antagonist needs to be constantly evolving so that the story remains flexible and fluid (and so that your markets expand). Don't create static stories. The one emotion you don't want your listeners to feel is boredom.

4. Having a good antagonist isn't only important in sales stories; it is even more important in the stories a company tells itself. If your team clearly understands what you are working to overcome—if the antagonist has been properly defined—and everyone is emotionally committed to overcoming it, your work is bound to be more alive and creative. Like the designers at Skunk Works, it might even become the stuff of legend.

5. Keep it real. If you don't, your own dark fantasies might come back to haunt you. If you do, you'll be amazed at what your antagonist has to say and teach.

Here is what we suggest you do. When you have a major presentation to make, rehearse it to understand its emotions as well as its content. You can't create emotions, but you can get comfortable revealing them, as long as you are aware that they are constantly shifting. What you feel as you give your talk one day might be totally different from what you feel another. So practice the entire range of emotions. For this, we suggest that you go out alone into nature. Someplace where you are not confined by walls. Someplace beautiful. Then run through this sequence.

- First, shout your pitch loudly and with enthusiasm, as if you are trying to get people in the back of a crowded bar to hear the good news.
- Then give it again, but this time, it is the funniest joke you have ever told. Let yourself laugh at the punch lines. Let yourself be silly and goofy.
- Then say it again, as you would to a lover. Be sentimental, be gentle, and make the story like a caress. It's OK. You're alone in the woods. You can be as sappy as you want. In fact, you should be even sappier. If it brings a tear to your eye and a tremble to your voice, so much the better.
- Now say it again, but this time it is dead-serious business and you are giving people orders that they have to understand. You are like a general speaking to your troops. Lives depend on what you have to say. You have to be clear and concise. They have to know what they are getting into, and how they are going to get out safely.
- Finally, tell it in a whisper. Like you are explaining it to a child as she is about to drift off to sleep and dream pleasant dreams. Make your voice inviting, a little hypnotic, and ever so safe.

After you have run through this sequence, forget about it. This is like the stretching a runner does before a race. When you are rehearsing, certain emotions may seem to go best with certain parts of your talk, but don't try to re-create those moments in the talk itself. If you stay loose and relaxed, you will see some of these voices coming up naturally as you speak. When they do, enjoy them. <u>The more you enjoy your talk, the more everyone else in the room will as well.</u>

CHAPTER EIGHT

Under the Radar

Let's say, just for the sake of argument, that you don't own your own television network, you aren't an A-list player with one of the big-three talent agencies, and you don't have an unlimited advertising budget. How are you, with just what you have right now—too little time, not enough money, but a really great idea—going to get the word out to a wide—even a worldwide—audience?

The short answer is that you turn to the person next to you and you start telling them your story. That's what Al Gore did twenty years ago, and now his story of global warming is on everyone's lips and is beginning to change the world. Your story can do the same thing. This whole book has been preparing you to do just that, and by now, believe us, you are good to go, particularly if you've been doing the suggested exercises along the way. But even if you haven't been doing those, don't worry, and don't wait. Just get started. You know you want to. You have something to say, so say it. People love to talk.

Word of mouth is the oldest and purest form of advertising. It still works, and everyone—particularly marketing professionals—knows it still works. JetBlue is one company that has built its success around a word-of-mouth strategy. You don't see a lot of ads for JetBlue; you do hear a lot of people talking about it. A word-of-mouth campaign is low cost and high touch. The advantages of low cost are obvious. Like they say, talk is cheap, but it is the high-touch part that interests us here. Because your story is actually being told from one person to the next, it isn't frozen in time the way it would be on TV or in print; it remains personal and flexible. As a result, word of mouth is much more likely to turn your story's negatives into positives than any other means of presentation. If you get the flow right, every person who passes your story along actually makes it just a little better.

As a major airline, JetBlue's story has one inherent negative. It doesn't always operate out of the major hubs. If you fly JetBlue out of Los Angeles, you actually have to catch the plane in Long Beach, which can add as much as forty-five minutes to your trip. If you find that out by reading an ad in the paper, it may register as a big "don't bother" and you might as well choose another airline, even if it costs a bit more. But if a friend tells you about Long Beach as he is describing his flight on JetBlue (and he enjoyed the flight), he will probably also tell you that Long Beach Airport is actually very charming, that security is quicker and much more pleasant than at LAX, and that traffic on the freeway wasn't nearly the hassle he thought it would be. Because you are hearing it from a friend, you start to see how going to Long Beach might actually be a positive. It might make your trip a little more fun and special.

JetBlue carries the personal feel of word of mouth into how it takes reservations. CEO David Neeleman pioneered a system that uses the Internet to link seven hundred reservation agents, allowing them to work from their home computers. This saves JetBlue a lot of money because it doesn't have to maintain an expensive twenty-four-hour call center, and the employees like it because it cuts down their commute time and makes work schedules more flexible. Many of these agents are stay-at-home moms who are keeping an eye on their kids as they help you book your ticket. When you call, you can sometimes hear children playing and laughing in the background—not an unpleasant sound. What you don't sense is that there is a supervisor looking over your agent's shoulder, keeping her to a predetermined script and glancing nervously at the clock. Your business is being dealt with as quickly and efficiently as it would be at any airline, but it all feels a lot more relaxed and welcoming. Of course it does. You're talking to a mom sitting at her kitchen table. What is more warm and welcoming than that? You don't need to be told that. It comes across in her tone of voice. And so what is often one of the negatives of your trip—making the reservation in the first place—becomes an opportunity for a positive and personal relationship with the airline. If you like the person you are talking to—if she really seems to be talking to you, not at you—then you are going to want to call back. Tone of voice is mostly what is carrying that message.

The human voice is by far the most powerful communication tool there is; direct personal contact is the best way to use it. So telling your story face-to-face really is the best way to get it across. But going door-to-door may not be the most efficient way to use your time, so it makes sense to construct your story in a way that compels other people to tell it for you. Whether you call this viral marketing, guerrilla marketing, or buzz marketing (all three terms mean essentially the same thing, but each emphasizes a different aspect of the technique—we'll see all three aspects as we go along), getting your story out this way is the penultimate accomplishment of the commercial storyteller's art. Why do the work yourself if you can get other people to enjoy doing it for you? Not only enjoy doing it, but actually pay you for the privilege.

A successful buzz marketing strategy is part carny hustle, part face-to-face street smarts (because it uses established social networks to spread the word, rather than trying to create its own unique fan base), and part Internet media mojo. Keeping the balance right is tricky, and there is no guarantee going into it that it will work. You could fall on your face, and you could fall hard. There has been no film in recent memory that had more advance buzz than *Snakes on a Plane*. Do you know anyone who will admit to actually buying a ticket to see it? We don't even know anyone who admits to renting the DVD. If your story doesn't have substance, buzz will not be enough. If people feel cheated by your story, the buzz will turn nasty. So before you decide to use this communication strategy, take a moment to be absolutely certain that your core story is solid. When buzz turns bad, it can be a quick ticket to oblivion, rarely giving you a second chance to get your story straight.

But that whiff of danger is actually a strong positive. This type of storytelling is all about awareness, the fourth of our five story elements and the one that corresponds to Air. As any rock climber will tell you, nothing makes you more aware of the world around you than being on the edge and letting it all hang out. You are close to the summit, the air is thin; take a deep breath and feel the way it makes your brain sparkle, because after this, it is an easy downhill run to the finish line.

Nothing spreads faster than a rumor. And nothing is harder to control. That is important to remember because there is an inherent negative bias in the way and speed with which buzz spreads. People who have a positive experience with your story will tell others about it an average of five to ten times. It just comes up in conversation. They enjoy doing it. It makes them feel as if they are in the know, and that they are doing you a favor by sharing something they value. But if their experience is negative, they will pass that along between seven and fifteen times. They are almost twice as likely to talk about it. And because when they do talk about it their conversation will carry a residue of negative emotional charge, it is more than twice as likely that you will remember it. So to keep your story on the tip of everyone's tongue *and* to keep it positive, it makes sense to talk to a professional about how to generate the right kind of buzz before you jump in over your head. This is like the part of a TV show where we say, "Kids, don't try this at home," except we want you to try it. It is more than worth the risk because it is low cost and high touch, because it is highly scalable, because people talking to each other about your ideas gives those ideas instant authenticity and street cred, and because figuring out ways to get them talking stimulates your own creative juices and makes your products and ideas better for the effort. Best of all, this sort of out-of-the-box storytelling is a lot of fun.

We do want to connect you with one of the best advisors we know before you do it, though, just to be on the safe side. See, this is viral marketing at work. We're telling you what one of our friends told us, and we're feeling good about doing it because we value what they said and we think it will help. We're passing on the buzz.

The best person at buzz we know here in LA—and LA is to buzz what Wall Street is to stocks and bonds—is Liz Heller, the founder and CEO of Buzztone. Like many of the best in this field, Liz comes out of the music business.

If you were in New York City a few Christmases ago, you

probably saw Liz spinning her magic. In fact, if you weren't paying attention, her story line might very well have run you over. Suddenly, Midtown Manhattan was filled with messengers in red and white sailor suits shooting up and down the streets on bright-red Vespa motor scooters delivering messages in bottles to the city's most influential trendsetters. The message: your ship has come in, don't miss out on a good thing.

The ship in question was a 220-foot barge, decorated with enormous red and white Target logos, which the Target chain was using as a pop-up store for Christmas shoppers. Pop-up stores—stores that arrive, stay briefly, then disappear—are an idea that is gaining traction as a marketing ploy. Architect Ron Pompei, who we'll meet in the next chapter, designed a particularly successful one for Levi Strauss. There is something intriguing about a store that appears and disappears like a dream. Done right, it catches your attention and you want to talk about it. The idea of pop-up stores around Christmas is already in many people's minds (as we'll see, viral marketing is most effective when it is confirming something we already know or suspect) because in malls all across the country specialized stores that sell Christmas decorations and wrapping paper suddenly come into existence around Thanksgiving, then just as ephemerally disappear after New Year's Day. But Target was taking a big risk by elevating the idea to a whole new level. It felt it had no choice.

For years, the major discount retailers—Target, Wal-Mart, J. C. Penney, Kmart—have been trying to break into the Manhattan market. Most have settled in for a long siege, building stores in the outer boroughs and slowly chipping away at Manhattan using their lower prices like a battering ram. Eventually, they are convinced the walls will fall. But Target, whose market niche emphasizes affordable, clever design, can't afford to wait that long. Manhattan's Seventh Avenue is America's design center. It is where the next generation of designers come to be trained. If Target has no presence in Manhattan, it stands a chance—a very good chance—of losing connection with the fashionista-on-the-cheap image that separates it from the rest of the big-box brands. Not today or tomorrow, but five or ten years from now, its whole branding effort could become passé; to guard against that, the company brought in its barge. It wasn't really there to sell product—though the company intended to sell as much as it could; the barge was there to sell Target's relevance to the next generation of New York's young and hip design trendsetters. Target could probably afford to write off the whole adventure as an advertising loss if it came to that. What it couldn't afford was the bad word of mouth that would be generated if it threw a big party and no one showed up. To make sure that it got the crowds it wanted, Target turned to Liz and Buzztone.

She was facing two major hurdles. It would be hard to find a more out-of-the-way place to put a store than the East River docks in winter, where it is typically cold, windy, and unpleasant. There would be no drop-by business. If people came to the barge, they would have to be actively looking for it. And Christmas was the one time of year that Target's distinctive red and white design motif wouldn't stand out. Billboards all over the city were saturated with images of Santa in his white-trimmed crimson suit, and red SUVs driving through the snow. Conventional newspaper advertising wouldn't help. Macy's and the rest of Target's local competition—a big reason it wasn't able to break into the Manhattan market in the first place—had those pages already locked up.

So Liz and her team came up with the Vespas, the messengers in red and white sailor suits, and the messages in a bottle. It worked. Before long, it wasn't just standing room only on the barge; there was a line extending far down the dock waiting for a chance to get in and join the claustrophobic crush (a 220-foot barge is a very large boat, but it is a very, very small department store). The barge was mentioned on all the morning talk shows—both local and national—and appeared in all the papers, including the *New York Times,* which has international reach. Liz's job was to make people aware that there was a Target barge docked on the East River and to get them talking about it, and pretty soon that is what everyone was doing. How and why her approach worked so well demonstrates the ways that the five story elements need to be harnessed by any successful viral marketing campaign.

Liz's job was to make people aware that Target was in town. Awareness at the level that we are now discussing takes place in the cerebral cortex—that area of the brain that is uniquely human and that has evolved so rapidly over the last 2 million years. If you are looking to change people's short-term behavior, this is where you need to focus, and pattern recognition is one of your best keys.

If you're out sailing, you scan the horizon for a certain type of ripple on the waves two hundred or three hundred yards away, knowing that when you see that pattern, it means wind will soon arrive. You can adjust the sails and be ready to take advantage of it. Your ancestors did the same sort of thing as they walked through the jungle scanning the foliage for patterns of movement. If they saw certain patterns, they took off running. They knew what was likely to come next and really wanted to be that crucial half step ahead of the tiger that would be chasing them. The ones who recognized the patterns first survived and multiplied. So we all have been bred to spend our lives scanning the world for clues to what comes next. Research has shown that people spend far more time thinking about the future than they do about either the present or the past. Makes sense; it is what they can actually do something about. If you want people to include your product or idea in their future, you need to give them a pattern they can recognize.

That is just what Liz was doing with all those red Vespa messengers. One wasn't a pattern. If one almost ran over you in a crosswalk, you would definitely remember it, but it wouldn't help mold or predict your future behavior. If you see two or three scooters, you will start to recognize a pattern. The way your brain is structured, you will start looking for more messengers so you can figure out what the pattern really means. You might be doing it unconsciously, but you will be glancing around. Five or six red and white sailors and the pattern becomes a puzzle, one that you can't quite stop thinking about. In fact, you might even dream about it at night. Being a social being, at some point you will turn to the person next to you and ask, "What's the deal with these sailors on the Vespas? And what is that in the bottle?" Buzz is starting.

When an asymmetric pattern has been set up, it almost has to create buzz. That is why the term we prefer for this type of marketing is "asymmetric advertising." Patterns, particularly incomplete patterns, can be almost irresistible. What you leave out in this type of communication is often more important than what you put in.

The incomplete nature of what you are trying to pass on is one reason that the term "viral marketing" is such a good one. A virus isn't trying to be a complete living cell. It is simply a piece of genetic material that gets into a living cell and hijacks it so it can spread. Liz wasn't trying to tell Target's complete story. That would have involved using the entire five-element model—establishing a point of view, an antagonist, all the rest. Not enough time to do it. All she wanted to do was get across one part of that story. The single story element that was crucial. In this case, it was "Target is in town," just that—the element of awareness. What Target is, what it can do for you, why you should care—all that she was leaving for you to fill in for yourself. She was counting on the fact that those ideas were already floating around in people's minds in the same way a virus is counting on the fact that the proteins floating around in a cell will be there when it needs them. Target is in town. That's all Liz was trying to get people to say. If it worked, pretty soon everyone would be saying it.

Why would they be saying it? Because it is fun. They would have figured out the answer to the puzzle of all those Vespas; and when they did, their brains would give them a shot of endorphins. It feels good to solve a puzzle. That's why crosswords are still in the paper. A side effect of endorphins is that they make you a little talkative, so you want to tell your friends what you just did. As we mentioned, viral marketing works across established social networks. Your friend needs to go shopping, too. Maybe you should head down to the barge together? And text messaging a few others to join you there doesn't seem a bad idea either. Because the message is so short and sweet—Target is in town—it can spread quicker than the flu.

We don't want to give you the impression that all Liz did was come up with the good idea of sailors on red Vespas, then sit back and trust to luck (though we will get back to just how good that idea was in a moment). Nothing could be further from the truth. A guerrilla marketing campaign is actually much more complex to mount successfully than the conventional approach. It has more moving parts, for one thing, and it needs to be watched very closely in order to maximize all the unforeseen but potentially very positive effects that thousands of largely unscripted conversations are generating. So there is more homework to be done. Before the first Vespa hit the streets, Buzztone had a Web site up and running (that's the Internet media mojo we mentioned), letting people know the best subway exits to take to get to the pier and trumpeting upcoming special events. Her cyber team was also getting the barge mentioned on all of the local shopping blogs and posting on all of the design-oriented chat rooms. To prime the crowd pump, she had set up a drawing that would give away a $1,000 gift certificate to one lucky hotel concierge chosen at random from those who sent guests down to Target to shop, and she made sure that all the major hotels had plenty of little maps to hand out if anyone asked where they should go to get a quick gift for the family back home. Her street team of good-looking shills—a team Buzztone has spent years putting together as Liz promoted bands and concerts in cities across the country—was prowling SoHo's see-and-be-seen bars spreading the good word late into every night. And, of course, like any LA buzzmeister, Liz already had the numbers of all the morning news show booking agents on her speed dial so she could call back quickly when she got the calls she knew they would be making to her to find out just what was going on. But she was careful not to let the media drive the story. The story was being told to one person at a time on the streets of Manhattan. She kept it that way because she knew that in this case the story *was* the buzz.

When you strip your story down to its elemental minimum and make it viral, every part of the core image becomes crucial. As Liz puts it, you need to "align your message, the medium, and the market." It is here, at the level of core image, that Liz really shows her brilliance. You may see it only for a moment driving by, but that sailor on the Vespa deconstructs in your mind into just the sentence she wants you thinking.

Take the red Vespa. The Vespa is widely recognized as one of the classics of modern industrial design. It is even part of the permanent display at the Museum of Modern Art, and it burns almost no gas, so it is a cheap way to get around town. That is the cheap and chic part of what she is trying to get across. That is the message.

Then there are the red and white sailor suits. Red and white, of course, connotes the Target brand, but it also links to Christmas, turning these sailors into Santa's aquatic little helpers. And there is more than a hint of the Village People in the image. If we are offending anyone, we apologize in advance, but there is something very fey in the whole red and white sailor suit thing. Before you think of us as being homophobic and overreacting, remember that this campaign was mounted in 2004, the year that *Queer Eye for the Straight Guy* won its Emmy and was the most talked about show on cable. That show was riding the whole "metrosexual" craze. Each week, a group of gay designers would give a heterosexual slob a total makeover, usually at the suggestion of his loved ones. It was aimed squarely at the very same demographic that Target was trying to attract with its barge, and it was turning into a product-placement bonanza for Bravo. So we don't think the reference was totally unintentional. It is always good to have a hint of taboo when you are building buzz. That is the market.

The medium is, of course, the message in the bottle that is actually inviting people down to the barge. It is in a bottle. It obviously comes from someplace far away and exotic. It probably tells you where you can go to find buried treasure—though this time X won't mark the spot; a big red and white Target bull's-eye will. Treasure hunts are fun, so instead of the long trek down to the docks being a hassle, it will be an adventure. The biggest negative of the barge-at-the-docks story is being directly addressed and converted into a positive.

Now that we have deconstructed the image, let's put it all together into a simple sentence (your brain does this automatically, by the way; you don't often think the sentence consciously, but research shows that it is in your mind some-where): "Cheap and classic design items that can help you change from a fashion loser to a fashion winner are waiting to be discovered down at the docks, and going there will be a lot of fun."

Liz never said that to you in so many words. You said it to yourself. That is why you value it. That is why you tell your friends. Imagine that she had put big red and white sandwich boards on the messengers reading, "Target has a store down on the East River with really cheap nice stuff. Come down and shop." Would that have made the same impression? Would it have made any positive impression at all? Not really. So, in asymmetric advertising, remember, less is always more.

And you can make that less almost nothing and still have tremendous impact. Guerrilla marketing techniques (this term is most often used in the political arena, where it emphasizes the technique's "under cover of darkness, strike where you least expected" quality) can be very powerful in political campaigns, but almost always as part of a last-minute negative attack. Rumors and buzz tend to trend negative, and negative buzz travels faster and hits harder than positive word of mouth, particularly if it is fueled with an active campaign like push polling. In push polling, voters get a call from a person who claims to be an objective pollster gathering information, but who is in fact working for one of the candidates (or their supporters) and is calling to put a viral message into our thinking. This is what happened to

John McCain during the 2000 Republican primary in South Carolina.

John McCain had easily won the 2000 primary in New Hampshire by almost 18 percent over George W. Bush. Going into the southern primaries, the Bush camp knew that if it didn't get a clear win, it was all over. So they were feeling a little desperate. On the days before the election, thousands of registered Republicans received calls asking them a few simple questions. Only three or four quick questions, because there were a lot of calls to make. And really only one mattered. That was the one that contained the virus "Would you be more likely or less likely to vote for John McCain for president if you knew he had fathered an illegitimate black child?"

He hadn't, of course. But then, no one said he had. The callers were just asking a hypothetical. To make things even more deniable, no one was quite sure who was making the calls. But like any good guerrilla campaign, this one depended on the voters putting facts they already had in their head together to produce the desired effect. John McCain and his wife, Cindy, *had* adopted a dark-complected daughter named Bridget from Mother Teresa's orphanage in Bangladesh and brought her to the United States for medical treatment, ultimately making her part of the family. It was a truly good and decent thing to do, the sort of thing campaign managers like to let people know their candidates do without making too much of it, so there were plenty of pictures out there of McCain with Bridget in his arms, smiling with fatherly pride.

To make sure people got the connection, a Bob Jones University professor named Richard Hand sent an e-mail to "fellow South Carolinians" stating that McCain had "chosen to sire children without marriage." When CNN confronted Professor Hand and asked what proof he had that McCain had fathered children out of wedlock, Hand responded, "Can you prove that there aren't any?" If it weren't so serious, it would have been comical—but it was serious. The election was fast approaching, and the damage had been done and just kept spreading. McCain lost the election badly, and you know the rest.

In line with what we have been saying about keeping what you say very short and sweet if you want to create buzz, this chapter has focused exclusively on how to use buzz or viral marketing to reach a mass audience. There is no cheaper and faster way. But the techniques of asymmetric storytelling are highly scalable. They can work just as well to get everyone within your company talking about your idea, as well as motivate people in a client company to pass along the buzz and help you make a sale. But because you are getting them to create the story in their own mind, they might not give you credit for it. As long as you agree with Costco CEO James Sinegal that there is no telling what you are capable of accomplishing as long as you are willing to let others take the credit for it, these are techniques you should try.

Before you do, you need to ask yourself if the story you have to tell lends itself to guerrilla marketing. If you can answer yes to the following questions, it probably does. If not, you may need to adjust your strategy until you get a yes.

1. *Is there a specific event that the buzz can cluster around?* People are much more likely to talk about something that actually exists in time and space. A ticking clock—something that requires action before a specific deadline—helps push things forward even more. The opening of a pop-up store, a planned vacation, a coming holiday, an approaching project deadline—all will get people primed to talk. If your story doesn't connect to an event, create one. That is what Liz did with the drawing for the concierges in the Target campaign. It got the concierges talking among themselves about the store down at the docks, which led to them passing out more invites.

2. *Is there already enough information in the minds of your audience for them to construct the story you want them thinking about?* The idea isn't just to get them talking, but to get them telling each other what you want them to say. If they don't have enough data to use a viral approach, start with conventional storytelling to get the ball rolling, then shift to a buzz campaign once the clouds have been seeded.

3. *Is there an element of taboo, controversy, or competition that you can link your buzz to?* Viruses are by nature opportunistic; that is what makes them spread so quickly. If people are already talking about something, and you can hook your idea to that, do it. And it works just as well if you can link your idea to something that is lurking around in their ids that they don't normally want to talk about. Sin prod-

ucts, like tobacco and alcohol, are traditional users of viral marketing techniques for this reason. Find a way to make your buzz both sexy and a hot topic.

4. *Do you know what single story element you need to get across in order to get the ball rolling?* You aren't trying to tell the whole story, just a single trigger piece of it. Usually *one* of the first four story elements (passion, hero, antagonist, awareness) will be enough to start the buzz *if it is the right one.* If the right one doesn't pop into your mind, then you aren't ready to use this technique for that idea. Relax. Wait for it, and chances are it will come.

5. *Is your target audience relatively defined, compact, and already self-identified?* Because you are going to set up a pattern, you need to have a sense of the edges that will contain it. You want to get your idea bouncing around, so you need to have walls for it to bounce off of. Midtown Manhattan was large enough so that lots of red Vespas could be launched into it, but compact enough so Liz could count on people seeing more than one or two of them in a day. A primary election works so well for a guerrilla marketing attack because the number of likely voters is relatively small and defined. This is all about the space in which the buzz you get going is likely to spread. Cyberspace works great here, so if you are aiming to communicate with a group that actively e-mails each other, this is a major plus. Groups that spend time around the watercooler are also good

vectors for infection. Remember, this style of story-telling uses established social networks. You aren't reinventing the wheel; you are just taking everyone out for a spin.

If you want to tune yourself up for this type of storytelling, here is a simple exercise we recommend.

Asymmetric storytelling is all about awareness. It is like a breath of fresh air. So, go out for a long walk: in the country, in a park, along the beach or mountain stream, or even on a busy city street as long as there aren't too many diesel fumes. Wherever you like to walk, walk there—but make sure it is someplace where the air is good, because you want to feel free to take a deep breath and soak it all in.

As you are walking, be aware of what is capturing your at-tention. Don't try to control what you are looking at; just be aware of what you find interesting moment to moment. You are just an observer, watching yourself watch the world.

Don't follow the thoughts that what you are noticing will be creating in your own mind. Just let those thoughts go, even the ones that seem really good. They'll still be there when you get back to them, but right now you are focusing on what captures your attention. This is an exercise, just like the others in this book. This one is about your awareness and what cap-tures it. Keep bringing yourself back to that. If you find it hard to let go of your thinking, take a deep breath and then let it go.

When you're ready, go on to the next step. Notice what

it is about what you are seeing that catches your attention. It will always be one of the basic story elements, because that is how your brain works. Which one is it?

For example, a young woman getting off a bus catches your eye. What is it about her that holds your attention? Specifically. Is it her vitality, her sexuality, the sense of passion she is bringing to the moment? Or is it the regal and heroic way she seems to control the territory around her? Maybe she's struggling to overcome some inner problem, or she's in a heated conversation with someone else, or there is a fluidity and direction to her movements that lets you know she is off to overcome an antagonist or obstacle. Maybe it is the way she is looking at something—her own awareness. Maybe she is looking back at you. Whatever it is, notice it, note it in your memory, and keep moving, letting your attention go to the next thing it finds fascinating on your journey. Then notice that, too, and be aware of what makes you notice it. Whichever element pops into your mind as you notice something is the one that makes that thing buzzable.

Do this for at least ten minutes, and do it for five days in a row. If you do, you will notice that your sense of the four elements sharpens. As a result, your use of them in storytelling will quickly improve.

CHAPTER NINE

The Storytelling Space

Stories don't exist in a vacuum; they always occur within a context. If you understand your story's context, it is much more likely that you will achieve the transformation you are aiming at. Transformation is, of course, our fifth and final story element. In commercial storytelling, which is the type we've been focusing on, transformation usually involves your getting paid. That is what this last chapter is all about. The big payoff.

Partially because this is a book, and so we are telling our story here through the medium of words linked lineally on a page, and partially because we are all predisposed to think of stories as things we tell to each other, it would be normal for you to assume that we see story primarily as words strung together. We don't. We are very aware that most of the stories we come into contact with every day aren't being told to us by people talking, but are being told silently by things simply being what they have been carefully designed to be. The can opener we use, the car we drive, the clothes we wear are all communicating with us through inherent story elements. If they didn't, we couldn't hold them in our minds long enough to buy and use them. As we hope we have made clear by now, that is how we are all wired.

Some of the most creative commercial storytelling being done isn't being done by the advertising industry, which at best can get us to make a trip to the store, but by the designers of the stores themselves, the spaces that actually help us buy products. No one creates these spaces better than Ron Pompei, the architect whose design team is behind the Urban Outfitters and Anthropologie retail stores.

The average American mall store sells $330 of product per square foot per year. An Anthropologie store sells over $800 of product per square foot. It can do this because the women who shop at Anthropologie visit more often and stay longer than at any other comparable chain. Ron and his design team create such a welcoming and creative environment by consciously using the same five story elements we have been discussing. His stated goal is to give visitors to Anthropologie "transformational experiences" by emphasizing what he calls the three "Cs": culture, commerce, and community.

Of the three, community is the one the Anthropologie

brand most emphasizes, but as its name implies, its corporate story is strongly rooted in a deep understanding of culture. As a culture, we are all moving through the transition from an industrial to a postindustrial economy—from an economy that was based on buying things to one that is based on buying experiences; experiences that we contain in ourselves as stories. We are moving from a time that valued high-status objects to one that values high-status experiences. Not so long ago, wearing an expensive watch to a party got you noticed the right way; now, to get the same attention, you need to mention your recent vacation to an eco-friendly resort in Brazil. How Ron and Anthropologie reflect this transformation in our buying patterns has a lot to say about what the future holds for us all.

Compare the experience of walking into a typical mall department store with walking into one of Ron Pompei's Anthropologies and you will see how he consciously uses the richness of the five story elements to create a sense of community. That sense of community naturally creates a wave of commerce that radiates out into our culture—his 3 Cs. You don't have to take our word for it. Anthropologie's estimated revenue in 2005 was more than $500 million, up from $350 million the year before, and the stock price of the parent company, Urban Outfitters (Ron also designs those stores), grew from $4.50 a share in 2000 to $27.50 in 2005, giving the company a market value of over $4 billion. Creating spaces where people can discover and share their own shopping stories is a very profitable business strategy.

As a creative architect, Ron is careful to design each of

Anthropologie's over eighty stores to be different. He doesn't want the stores to seem like a chain; he wants each customer's experience to be authentic and unique. As he says, "You wear totally different clothes in Seattle than you do in New York City, so why would a store in one place look like a copy of one in the other?"

Because each of his store designs is so different, we'll use the Anthropologie that just opened near us as an example. It is in an upscale-lifestyle mall called The Grove in Los Angeles. But if you go to the Anthropologie nearest you—there is a very interesting one that just opened in Rockefeller Center in Manhattan—you will see the same principles at work.

Because we are now dealing with nonverbal storytelling, it is good to remember Empedocles' original elements. The ideo-tropic nature of the Greek elements makes them very visual and evocative, and they resonate in us at a deep psychological level. Once again, they correspond directly with our five story elements: passion = Fire, hero = Earth, antagonist = Water, awareness = Air, transformation = Space.

When you walk into the Anthropologie at The Grove, the first impression you get is of space—free, open space, and lots of it. The ceiling is over thirty feet above your head, but it is there. You aren't outside, but you also aren't inside a room with anything like normal proportions either. It is more like stepping into a cathedral than it is like stepping into a store where every cubic inch of space is usually dedicated for just one thing—shelf space. We'd say that the effect you feel on entering is slightly disorienting—it definitely signals that something unusual is about to happen in this store—except that the experience is so extremely oriented. It is just that instead of being focused on the buying opportunity the store is currently pushing some twenty feet away and off to your right—as it would be in a typical mall store—Ron's design is orienting you to look up. And you do. It is uplifting. You slow down, your spine straightens, you stand just a little taller, you look up, and you take a deep and relaxing breath. At least we did when we entered, and so did almost all the people who came in during the ten minutes after us, who we observed at Ron's suggestion. They straightened, they looked up, and then took a deep, relaxing breath.

What they were looking up at was a huge circular chandelier of the style found in many Middle Eastern mosques. The store's name—Anthropologie—is well chosen. The chain's CEO, Richard Hayne, is a trained anthropologist, and before opening the first store (he had already established Urban Outfitters), he and Ron spent two years traveling the world visiting sites of interest, studying sacred spaces and discovering artifacts that spoke to them. Many of their experiences are reflected in the individual store designs. The chandelier at The Grove store has five concentric rings of lit globes (here lit by electric lights, but in its original incarnation these glass globes were lit by dishes of burning oil) suspended twenty feet above us.

Ron introduces the stories this Anthropologie will contain by revealing the element of fire. It is the first of our five elements, and it is the first thing you encounter on entering the store. Like fire always does, it motivates you. The chandelier's concentric circular pattern motivates you to move around. It isn't pulling you forward to a predetermined sales station; it is simply suggesting in strong visual terms that you take some time, walk around, and explore. And people do. The average stay in an Anthropologie store is a leisurely seventy-five minutes (the stay in a typical mall store is around twenty-two).

The earth beneath our feet echoes the idea of walking around. The floor at the entranceway is brown-toned concrete with raised circular ridges. If like us you are wearing thick-soled walking shoes, you can feel those ridges, but the effect is subtle. However, the target demographic of Anthropologie is successful women in their thirties and forties, college educated, who have already finished the mating dance and are now looking to feather their nest with interesting and authentic items of real value. These women are much more likely to be wearing fashionable shoes with thin leather soles, and so are far more likely to perceive the message in the concrete—walk around, explore, this is a highly textured space filled with surprises. Ron has carefully aligned the elements of earth and fire.

We asked Ron how he used the element of water. He said that for him it was all about the flow of customers, which he intentionally keeps very unstructured. Clothing isn't arranged on racks in straight lines along aisles. Instead, the floor pattern resembles eddies in a river. There is no one way to get across the room. Whatever way you take will be a bit of an adventure, with products of the strangest types suddenly coming into view: books on Italian villas, a set of martini glasses with a chrome shaker, or our favorite (which we found in the Anthropologie in Manhattan)—a small, out-of-the-way room filled with sculptures that resembled alien fish heads made from colorfully painted motorcycle gas tanks. These little discoveries are all objects telling stories by simply being what they are. <u>Each discovery creates a separate moment of awareness and makes us want to see and experience more.</u> <u>That is the essence of good design.</u> And good design at an Anthropologie is contagious.

Though the store's floor pattern is open ended, it is not without direction. Like a river, it flows downhill, from the high-vaulted entranceway across the main room, where a post and beam arcade about fifteen feet overhead meanders across the space, suggesting a direction for moving without in any way compelling us to follow it, to the lower-ceilinged and much more intimate dressing rooms in the back of the store. The dressing rooms, and the open space in front of them, are where women discuss with each other how they look and where they begin their "conversation" with the products they will decide to buy and take home. It is the dressing rooms that are the focus of an Anthropologie. They are the storytelling space within the store's larger story space, the soul of each Anthropologie. It is where the bonding of community occurs and from which it spreads. The cash registers, which are left off to the side of the main room, seem almost an afterthought.

How much of an afterthought is illustrated by a story Anthropologie's president Glen Senk tells about a star employee who would unfailingly sell $6,000 to $7,000 of merchandise in every three-hour shift. To find out how she did it, Senk observed her in action. What he saw was that she was a great salesperson who could sell almost anything, but "she really didn't care what she was selling so long as she made the sale. She was letting people walk out of the dressing room with things that simply didn't look good." He fired her immediately. As Ron told us, "If you help a woman find a pair of pants that really fit, you make a customer for life. She becomes part of your brand's community. If you treat her like a friend, you'll have one." The design of the store is all about providing each customer the space to do just that—to become a lifelong friend.

By providing all of these unstructured story elements and letting people construct their own stories out of them, Ron's design has converted Anthropologies from being providers of prepackaged shopping stories (in essence, the tagline at the end of the commercial that dragged you out to the mall in the first place) into being containers of totally original, always changing, constantly current shopping discoveries, each told as a story coauthored by one of the store's customers and hot off the presses.

Anthropologie never, ever advertises. It doesn't need to. Like any author, its customers take pride in their discoveries and share what they have learned with their friends. It isn't unusual to find women posting pictures of what they found on a day's trip to Anthropologie on their Web sites or on design and shopping blogs, or sending photos to a friend by way of their mobile phone—with a few choice words texted in for good measure. There is something about the authentic and highly textured quality of a trip to Anthropologie that makes it a nice fit with digital media. Like Google, Anthropologie is all about finding what you are looking for, having fun doing it, and linking with others along the way.

The hunger for discovery that keeps shoppers looking through an Anthropologie longer than they do in an average store is also fueling a tremendous growth spurt in museums. In 2006, 86 of the 175 museums that responded to a survey by the Association of Art Museum Directors said they were planning—or already involved in—expanding. They need to. Global attendance at art exhibitions increased by 21 percent from 2003 to 2004 alone, and attendance at New York's Museum of Modern Art—long an established cultural icon— has increased more than 100 percent since 1995, requiring a complete rebuild.

The building boom isn't restricted to art museums. Perhaps the most impressive museum rebuild currently going on is the one being done by the California Academy of Sciences. The academy is the second-oldest such institution in the United States. Members of the academy were with Darwin as he made the voyage that led him to his theory of evolution, and they were arriving back in San Francisco harbor with samples from the Galápagos when the great fire of 1903 broke out and burned much of the city to the ground.

When the museum decided to modernize and expand, its funders—largely philanthropists associated with Silicon Valley and the Internet boom of the late 1990s—wanted to make sure that the design was experiential and well integrated with the latest technology. With their corporate reputations on the line, they can't afford to be connected with anything stodgy. The old-style museum, with its endless collection of bugs all neatly cataloged in closed display cases, was the last thing they wanted to be associated with. They are movers and shakers in a world where information is intimate and immediate. They are looking to increase student interest in science for a very practical reason—they need the best and brightest young people to become engineers and scientists so that their workforce maintains its cutting edge. They need a museum that is hands-on and user friendly. So instead of turning to the usual suspects, the California Academy of Sciences looked to industrial design teams and commercial architects to create a space that would be a marketplace of competing ideas.

To do this, the academy brought in a half dozen of the world's best design teams and asked them to work together. It was a good idea, very creative, very much oriented toward creating spontaneous discoveries. Unfortunately, it was difficult to pull off in practice. These teams were used to competing with each other for jobs, not to cooperating on a common goal. They were the best at what they did, so each team had a strong and definite point of view on how to do it and didn't want to take the time to explain it to anyone else. Each team had its own unique corporate culture and its own design vocabulary. Their design concepts were different, and so was the language they used to describe them. To help deal with these problems, our consulting firm, FirstVoice, was called in.

We realized that our job was simple: to get these designers

telling stories. What they told stories about wasn't the most important thing; it was the storytelling itself that would bring them together. It always does—whether it is around a campfire in the woods, around the watercooler at the office, or in the dressing rooms of an Anthropologie. Once people start telling stories, they naturally create a common culture. But in this case, we wanted them to tell stories that would relate to the designs they would eventually be creating. Stories rooted in nature.

So after a brief introduction and a discussion of where we thought the project was at and where they thought it was going, we had two tables covered with sheets rolled into the room. It was around 10:30 AM, and the designers naturally thought we were about to break for coffee. When we pulled back the sheets, we revealed that the tables were actually covered with specimen jars of living bugs: two Mexican tarantulas, several vinegar bugs, a collection of flesh-eating beetles, and one lonely and lovely—but nonlethal—rock scorpion. To fill out the tables, we also included some mounted specimens of butterflies, wasps, and crickets. We asked the designers to take ten minutes to carefully observe the bug they felt most attracted to or repelled by. Bugs are a lot like stories. They are everywhere, and they are fascinating. The closer you study them, the more fascinating they become. We all studied the bugs together in silence.

Then we asked the designers to tell us a story from their own lives involving a bug. Stories poured out. Several people talked about being bitten by red ants as children. One architect told us about a butterfly that suddenly landed on her hand for no reason. We learned about a pet cricket that was kept inside a child's desk at school until one day it mysteriously disappeared. About scary spiders, hairy spiders, and rooms filled with spiderwebs. The stories just kept coming. An hour later when we broke for lunch, they were still pouring out, and the sense of community among the design teams was becoming firmly established. Stories build unity. It is what they do best.

When we came back from lunch, we took things to the next level. After explaining our five-element narrative model and how it might relate to museum installations, we divided the designers into teams of five (not the design teams they came with) and handed out photos of skulls from the museum's collection, asking each team to create a theater piece that would tell us a story using that skull as a mask. By asking for a theatrical presentation, we were getting them to move out of their normal style of visual expression and widening their storytelling vocabulary, making spontaneous discoveries more likely. Their theater pieces were amusing, occasionally touching, and always a lot of fun. Fun isn't extraneous to the discovery process. It is very much a part of maximizing the profits that discoveries contain. For years, cognitive psychologists have known that being happy actually makes you smarter.

In one classic experiment, psychologist Alice Isen showed people one of two films. One was neutral, the other a comedy that was fun to watch. Then she asked both groups to perform a creative task. She gave them each a box of tacks, a book of matches, and a candle and asked them to attach the candle to a corkboard wall in such a way that it could be lit. A classic design problem. Of the group that had seen the neutral film, less than 20 percent could solve the problem in ten minutes. But 75 percent of those who watched the comedy could solve it in the time given. She concluded, and subsequent experiments confirmed, that happiness positively affects cognitive functioning and actually makes our brain more flexibly organized. That is important to remember if you are working with a creative team.

One exhibit at the California Academy of Sciences's temporary installation in downtown San Francisco deserves special mention. Designed by Jonathan Katz, it is a wall of seal skulls arranged in what looks like a wave. It is one of the best examples of discovery stories told by objects that we know of— elegant in its simplicity. The series of skulls mounted on the wall represents the evolution of the modern seal. In front of this wall are three small display plaques that tell how the evolutionary pressures of their aquatic environment and choice of food have shaped the modern seal's skull. But one skull on the wall is not a seal skull. That skull is the skull of a fox. It is almost the same size. You have to look closely to see the differences. Viewers are challenged to find the skull that doesn't fit. To do it, they need to start thinking like scientists: comparing differences in the location of nostrils, the size and curve of incisors, and the shape of the skull itself, looking to find the pattern underneath. When they do that, they quickly find the fox skull and deeply enjoy making the discovery.

Putting people inside a discovery-containing space—making their experience of the museum creative and inter-active—is the main goal of the new museum complex now being constructed. Its signature centerpiece will be the world's largest enclosed rain forest. Designed by Pritzker Prize–winning architect Renzo Piano, this installation will be in a climate-controlled ninety-foot glass dome extending up more than four stories. Visitors will enter at ground level into a forest floor teeming with life—over sixteen hundred live ani-mals are part of this installation, including over a hundred exotic reptiles and amphibians, a cave full of bats, and even a three-toed sloth. As they move up a ramp and into the forest canopy above, they will observe trees from the rain forests of Borneo, Madagascar, Costa Rica, and the Amazon Basin and see more than thirty varieties of orchids growing as if in the wild. The air around them will be filled with life as well—more than six hundred species of free-flying birds and butterflies will swoop around them. A specially designed misting system will keep everything moist and happy, and the dome's skylight surface will allow the sun's natural life-giving fire to shine down on it all. Once they reach the top of the dome, visitors will take an elevator down and be suddenly plunged into the underwater world of the flooded Amazon rain forest, moving through a glass tunnel that allows them intimate views of the South American fish in the museum's one-hundred-thousand-gallon tank in as close to their natural habitat as can be provided.

If you are keeping track of the elements, this trip took each visitor from the earth teeming with life, into the air filled with birds and butterflies, stopped briefly to look down from the sun-sparkled dome (the sun is the source of all the fire in our ecology), then plunged us into an underwater world of a type we have never seen before. All four elements are covered, and all are designed to stimulate discoveries. There is no way, *no way*, kids visiting won't be transformed by the experience. And because they have been, and because they are kids, they are going to want to let all their friends know all about it. Not later, but right now—which they will do digitally. They all have cell phones; they all know how to use them. As any high school teacher will tell you, it is almost impossible to keep students from using them. Many will post images and stories on the Internet. Over 57 percent of teens who use the Internet are content providers (and that percentage is growing rapidly). Eighty-five percent of college students communicate across Facebook alone. That portal will change, but the desire to share stories digitally won't. A wave of stories is about to break in San Francisco, created by the experience-rich context of the new museum and promoting a culture that values the fun and excitement of scientific discovery. Exactly what all these stories will produce is impossible to predict, but it will be positive and, for someone (or someones), it will be very profitable. The information-age funders of the new home of the California Academy of Sciences are going to get more than their money's worth. The commercial potential of creating a storytelling space and then having people pay you to use it certainly extends into cyberspace. That is all YouTube is, after all, and Google just paid $1.8 billion for it! That is a success story in anybody's book.

* * *

At the end of each chapter, we have been giving you simple exercises to do. Here is the last one.

When we reach this point, our clients often say to us that they now know how to tell a story, but ask how they can find the right story to tell, one that is totally their own.

We began this book looking at how the ideas of the ancient Greek philosopher, Empedocles, impact modern cognitive psychology and narrative theory, so it seems appropriate to end with the words of another ancient philosopher, this one from the other side of the world, the tenth-century Kashmiri philosopher Tilopa.

Speaking to a student who was wrestling to make sense of an extremely complicated philosophic problem (and was experiencing a mental agony not that different from the headache you and I get when we dive into a pile of marketing and demographic data in search of a new sales angle), Tilopa offered this advice:

> Let go of what has passed.
> Let go of what may come.
> Let go of what is happening now.
> Don't try and figure anything out.
> Don't try to make anything happen.
> Relax, right now, and rest.

When you need to find the right story, you should follow his advice. Really, just sit back, close your eyes, and do what he suggests. In sequence. First, consciously let go of the past. You don't need to think about that now. Then let go of what might come, and on through the remaining steps Tilopa suggests. Finally, you will arrive at the moment when you relax and really rest. Enjoy it. Bask in it. And notice, without thinking about it, that when you look out at the inside of your eyelids, your mind is filled with a delicate luminous glow. Nothing special. It is always there. And in a moment, without your doing anything, a story will come. It always does. If it is a good story, if it makes you happy, tell it to someone.

So, to sum it up—to sum it all up.

1. Stories are facts wrapped in emotions, not just facts alone. People tell stories because that is how they view and understand the world. Telling them stories, and listening to and responding to theirs, is the best way to promote your products, services, and ideas. If you do that, you will stay in business; if you don't, you won't. It really isn't much more complicated than that. Stories are the irreducible core, the fire, inside every business. And telling stories doesn't have to be frightening. We can all learn to do it professionally. It is what we are doing every day anyway.
2. Every story contains five story elements.
   - The *passion* or energy with which you tell it.

- The *hero* who gives your story a point of view and allows your audience to enter into the story.
- An *antagonist*—or obstacle—that presents problems that must be overcome. It is the struggle with this problem that generates the emotions the story contains, and allows us not only to enter the story, but also lets the story become part of us.
- A moment of *awareness* that reveals itself and allows us to learn from the story and so succeed.
- A *transformation* that occurs because of what you—represented by the hero—have done. Things are different, and usually better, because of the obstacles overcome and discoveries made. People love happy endings. For that reason, we want to pass the story on.

3. Knowing these five elements and using them to your best advantage will make your stories more focused, effective, and profitable. Why would you do anything else? To make them easy to remember, we often call this our PHAAT model (pronounced "fat"; think of an obese, mega-successful hip-hop star resplendent in bling bling rapping out his rhyming story line). *P*assion, *H*ero, *A*ntagonist, *A*wareness, *T*ransformation. PHAAT. It is a model that works. Use it.

4. The most delicate parts of your story, its most fragile components, are the emotions it contains. These are also its most important parts. Facts without emo-

tions are dry, lifeless, and not long remembered. Stories take on a life of their own. It is common in many businesses to be told not to be too emotional. We agree, you shouldn't be hysterical, but emotions are part of how we think, and not using your entire thinking on a subject of importance is most often a mistake. We are all shy. We have all been hurt by having our feelings rejected. Be of good heart. Push forward and tell the whole truth. You will be glad you did. And to be sure that it is heard in the way you intended, place it in a good story.

5. Stories are everywhere. Just look around. Anything that captures your attention contains a story. If it is a man-made object, that story was probably put there intentionally. Enjoy it. If it is something in nature, the story it contains is yours to discover. You may be the first one to find it. It is inspiring to see the world this way, glittering with light and freshly exposed. It is also highly profitable.

6. Stories, just by being stories that are told, create communities. Culture and commerce are the inevitable result. People have been telling each other stories since they gathered around the first campfires—and probably long before that. It is wired into our genes. It is what makes us human. As social beings, the culture we live in is an intricate net of shared stories, and as the world shrinks and becomes more and more transnational, moving inevitably toward the time when human culture will be one, the stories

we choose to tell each other become more and more important. We can no more separate ourselves from our storytelling than fish can separate themselves from water. But if we know and use the five elements of storytelling, we can become the big fish.

When that happens for you, when you are the one sitting at the head of the boardroom table, what sort of stories will you tell? We hope that you will use your position to create a storytelling space, one where everyone's stories can be heard. It's the smart move to make. You might have the best ideas in the room—you probably do—but if they are the only ideas expressed, you won't have fully harnessed the creative power of your team, and that is what big fish are there to do. When it is time to make the decision, communicate it through story. That way, your idea will be completely understood and absorbed. Howard Gardner, a professor of cognitive psychology at Harvard and the winner of a MacArthur grant for his work with multiple intelligences, puts it succinctly: "Every great leader is a great storyteller."

FURTHER READING

....

The Art of War, Sun-Tzu
Miyamoto Musashi: His Life and Writings, Kenji Tokitsu
Speaker Survival Guide, Deborah Shames and David Booth
⚹ *The Essays of Warren Buffet: Lessons for Corporate America*,
    Warren Buffett
Leading Minds, Howard Gardner
Memory and Emotion: The Making of Lasting Memory, James
    L. McGaugh
Rhetoric, Aristotle
From Metaphysics to Protoanalysis, Oscar Ichazo
⚹*The Tipping Point, How Little Things Make a Big Difference*,
    Malcolm Gladwell
Wabi-Sabi, Leonard Koren
Design Like You Give a Damn, Architecture for Humanity

INDEX